"*A Shaman's Tale* is a profound book that offers the reader both the opportunity to experience the author's personal journey and insights and provides a doorway to their own transcendent awakening."

— Martin Fiebert, Ph.D. Professor of Psychology, California State University, Long Beach

"Richard Alaniz, in sharing his life journeys with us, including experiences with his Apache teachers, opens up a fascinating landscape where each of us can let go of the erroneous beliefs that keep us small and separate, connect with the powers of the spiritual world, and walk this same path ourselves. Our fears of death have become our fears of life. In recognizing the continuity that links the worlds together, we learn to let go of them both, and find the spirit walker within."

— Kiara Windrider, Author, *Year Zero: Time of the Great Shift*, and *Ilahinoor: Awakening the Divine Human*

"Inspiring and life-changing wisdom, *A Shaman's Tale* provides the reader with a unique perspective in fulfilling their spiritual consciousness. Over the years, Richard has shared his insights with many, which enabled them to move forward in life. In gratitude, thank you Richard for sharing all that you know... creating a world for the best and highest good of all."

— Al Diaz, Author, *The Titus Concept: Money for My Best and Highest Good*, *Being the Titus Concept*, and *Confirmations*

"In Richard Alaniz's book *A Shaman's Tale*, the author and spiritual counselor poses a Psychospiritual Psychology, a synthesis of science and mysticism. Useful tools are given to discover spirit as a guide in walking our individual paths. Alaniz's own humanity inhabits his writing as he shares a visitation from his departed father. He tells us that it was this encounter from the other side that inspired his book. It is indeed refreshing to read such a book written not as academic theory but as life experience from one who has himself walked the path. In this way, the world is healed one individual, one tribe at a time."

— Catherine Ann Jones, Author, *Heal Your Self with Writing* and *The Way of Story*

"Mr. Alaniz does an outstanding job of presenting some very difficult material in his book *A Shaman's Tale*. He takes his readers along with him through his self-discovery of spirituality by way of his profound supernatural experiences. In following his journey readers will learn valuable tools to connect to their own spirit consciousness within their own lives."

— Wanda Chavez, Spiritualist

"Well worth reading as I could identify with his experiences. Kudos to the author for telling his tale in a way that embraces the reader so that we feel we are on the journey with him."

— Kaleo Paik, Traditional Hawaiian Cultural Practitioner

"Incredible, refreshing — a must-read that contrasts various beliefs and builds compelling arguments that leave the reader in total awe!"

— Karyn Reece, Psychic Medium, *www.karynreece.com*

"From Hollywood stuntman to shaman, Richard Alaniz crosses borders and blurs boundaries, taking the reader on a personal and compelling quest for greater wisdom. By stripping away the need for and dependence upon organized religions, he frees the individual to explore and be open to moving to a higher turn of the spiral of their own awareness. He continually assures that 'love vs. fear' is the best way to go, for everything. Billions of people believe in ghosts, exoplanet visitors, demons, vampires, etc., and lots of fear surrounds those concepts. His countering perspective can go a long way to bringing about more critical thinking."

— Pamela Jaye Smith, Mythologist, International Speaker-Consultant, Award-winning Producer-Director. Author of *Inner Drives, Power of the Dark Side, Symbols.Images.Codes, Beyond the Hero's Journey,* and *Show Me the Love!*

A SHAMAN'S
TALE

PATH TO SPIRIT CONSCIOUSNESS

RICHARD L. ALANIZ

DIVINE
ARTS

Published by DIVINE ARTS
DivineArtsMedia.com

An imprint of Michael Wiese Productions
12400 Ventura Blvd. #1111
Studio City, CA 91604
(818) 379-8799, (818) 986-3408 (FAX)

Cover Design: Johnny Ink. www.johnnyink.com
Book Layout: William Morosi
Copyeditor: Gary Sunshine
Printed by McNaughton & Gunn, Inc., Saline, Michigan

Manufactured in the United States of America

Library of Congress Cataloging-in-Publication Data

Alaniz, Richard L., 1951-
  A shaman's tale : path to spirit consciousness / Richard L. Alaniz.
    pages cm
  Includes bibliographical references and index.
  ISBN 978-1-61125-019-0
1. Parapsychology. 2. Occultism. 3. Spirituality. 4. Psychology. I. Title.
  BF1999.A585 2013
  131--dc23

                          2013015291

Printed on Recycled Stock
Publisher plants 10 trees for every one tree used to produce this book.

In memory of my father, Gilbert Z. Alaniz, who gave me my
greatest gift in life, by appearing to me two months after
his passing, effecting a life-changing experience;
and to my mother, Margie Alaniz, for without her nurturing guidance
and unconditional love I would not have survived the traumas of war.

Contents

PART I
PSYCHOSPIRITUAL PSYCHOLOGY: PATH OF PERSONAL DISCOVERY

PART II
KARMONIC EXPERIENCE: PERSONAL LIFE PLAN FOR SPIRITUAL CONSCIOUSNESS

PART III
THE PROBLEM WITH BELIEF SYSTEMS — AND HOW TO MOVE BEYOND

PART IV
FEAR VS. LOVE: THE ONLY REAL DECISION YOU'LL EVER NEED TO MAKE

Preface

This book was written for those who are interested in spirit consciousness, the paranormal, and how one engages with multidimensional spirit entities from the perspective of mysticism and shamanism. During many years of training as a shaman with the Mescalero Apaches and other indigenous cultures I decided to pursue an academic endeavor with the ultimate and final goal of an advanced degree in psychology. I rationalized that if I wanted mainstream society to take my work seriously — effects of spirit consciousness within human behavior — I would need to subject myself to the grueling task of institutionalized academia.

I applied and was accepted to California State University, Long Beach (CSULB). I chose CSULB for its excellent undergraduate program in psychology and to study under Dr. Mike Connor and Dr. Martin Fiebert, both my mentors and excellent professors at CSULB. My postgraduate plans were to either continue at CSULB or to attend New Mexico State University for a PhD in Counseling Psychology.

My work as a spiritualist, spiritual counselor, and academician in psychology set the foundation for the development of my theory of "Psychospiritual Psychology" and the idea of "Nature, Nurture, and Spirit." This theory, with no measurable value according to the scientific community, was the basis of my quest. Although there is a growing interest in transpersonal psychology for further research development in the area of spirituality and paranormal psychology, it is not fully accepted by the conservative majority.

Although the scientific community would label my practice as nonscientific, perhaps a form of witchcraft, I feel the future will usher in a synthesis of science and mysticism in defining the human psyche and the supernatural. The focus of my methodology allowed me to approach psychology from a different perspective. Eventually, the name "Psychospiritual Psychology" evolved to represent my life's work in the effects of spirituality on human behavior.

I consider myself a spiritual counselor; however, because of the method I developed to aid my clients, some more closely identified me as a holistic therapist, spiritual guide, or even a modern *curandero*. My methodology synthesizes indigenous shamanistic healing practices and modern psychological theories, to include the philosophies of Carl Jung, Carl Rogers' and Abraham Maslow's approach to humanistic psychology, psychodrama and Gestalt therapy.

My experiences with the paranormal and multidimensional entities have brought me to a realization that there is far more to life as we know it. We have been sidetracked to not see the realities beyond this dimension as we enforce religious belief systems to answer our questions about the spiritual world. Mystics throughout the centuries tell us of multidimensional worlds, yet science keeps us from investigating that possibility since the idea is categorized as philosophical. You will find that I am not asking anyone to consider this writing as a new belief system, but I do ask my readers to be open and to think critically.

I have discovered through meditation one can connect with a higher source (spirit guide) if an individual chooses to explore his/her inner self. By doing so, one can learn to connect the personality to the Spirit-self (soul, inner spirit) to find inner peace and an enhanced understanding through awareness. The Spirit-self, the eternal you, is connected to the essence of what many call "God."

My writings may seem to denounce and perhaps be irreverent toward belief systems. However, my intent is to offer an idea that is beyond current ideologies and to investigate the possibility that individuals are capable of reaching a higher consciousness. I do respect all religious perspectives; however, it is my duty to express what has been given to me. I wish not to offend or change the minds of others but merely to bring critical thinking skills to those who are caught up in belief systems and are in search of ideas outside of dogma. It is not the religion that I denounce; it is the inflexible belief system used to control, which blinds many from truth. I feel there is not one true religion — they are all paths *originally* constructed to offer guidance with beneficial teachings to advance human nature.

You will find that I redefined spirituality and offer a different perspective about the supernatural while shedding light on the extraterrestrial phenomenon and its connection to spirituality. Without moderation I submit myself as a witness.

Introduction

Within this book I provide anecdotes of my path to spirit consciousness and my paranormal experiences dealing with interrelated supernatural events. Two chapters, "The Five Ways of Knowing" and "The Power of Thought," each analyze how we think and why we believe in what we believe. However, the main theme in this book is to replace the struggle of *Good vs. Evil* with *Love vs. Fear* in order to offer a design for personal healing in eradicating fear from your thoughts, and to aid you in your own path to a higher spiritual awareness.

The idea for this book originated with a profound experience on the night of November 18, 2002, when I awoke from a sleep state around 11:00 p.m. At the time I considered the experience as just another message from my spirit guide because it was compelling. However, I was wondering why I was suddenly compelled to declare myself an author. Me, of all people — I was perplexed.

I was awakened for the second time that night at or about 1:30 a.m., and the title of the book was clearly given to me. My intention was to simply get out of bed, find my way to the computer, and write the title, which was what had just come to me in my silent voice. Three hours later I had recorded all the information that just kept flowing through my fingers and onto the keyboard, surprisingly visible as a rough outline. I was in awe to find this book would be about spirituality and my paranormal experiences that I long ago decided I would never share with others out of fear of being stigmatized.

I discovered I had a paranormal life starting at the age of five, and this "secret" life continued through my involvement with the Discovery Channel's production about the paranormal called *X-Ops* (filmed in November of 2005). I had always been grateful for the gift of knowledge that had been given through my paranormal experiences, and I now realized it was time to expose my life and put it in words for others to criticize.

My intention is to guide those who are seeking knowledge into a realm that at times may sound unbelievable. That is the purpose... for you to personally question and to hopefully awaken your mind to the possibility of another awareness that is dormant within you.

Awareness can come in a variety of forms, especially if one is open. When we are in the midst of a personal crisis we either attribute the circumstances to bad luck, or if we are religious, to God's will. In either case, we harbor thoughts of bitterness and feel we are not in control. We fall prey to fear and pessimism. Our "awareness" guides us away from the negativity, toward the idea that everything is for a reason. Those reasons support what I have termed "Karmonic Experience," a predestined life plan that is written in order for us to reach a higher level of spiritual consciousness within each incarnation.

A profound life-lesson that I have learned is that death is an illusion. In reality, death gives birth to life; it is a function of renewal of the supreme you. Who we really are does not experience death. We are eternal and timeless beings within a continuum of spirit consciousness.

This book describes my life path toward a *knowing* of truth through experiences that are void of *belief*. It is a path that I have endured, and my words will serve as road signs to hopefully motivate you to seek your own personal truth and awareness through *knowing*.

The concept of "belief" is disturbing to me. It separates humanity at the core and is troublesome for human potential. I prefer to "know," and by doing so I have no need for belief.

For some the search for inner peace is continually observed with the vision and mindset that one must find it in a non-Western philosophy such as Native American or Eastern religions. Many will believe it is necessary, because they feel there is importance in attaining a form of "power" and/or "wealth" to get what they want as one relates to inner peace, but in reality the ultimate truth is not there — it is within you.

There are benefits in learning from another culture, but you must relinquish your own belief system and personal philosophy. Once you are able to do this, you will have to live and learn the customs, history, language, superstitions, and social-cultural constructs of those you wish to learn from. In doing so, you will be able to view from the perspective from which the teaching was created to enrich that culture.

I visited twice a year, for over thirty years, with Apache people, learning their medicine ways. Before I started my apprenticeship as a shaman I learned the culture and social constructs of reservation life. Even though I am of Mexican and Comanche heritage, I still had to acculturate in order to think as an Apache and to see from within instead of observing from the outside. By definition in Apache culture I will always be an *outsider* — I just don't have to think like one.

You will see the term "Spirit-self" often. I use it to represent the truth of who you really are. It is the spirit energy, the spirit continuum, which exists in life and after death. It is the source of internal life energy that is represented in China as *Chí*, in India as *Prana*, in Hawaii as *Mana*, and in Japan as *Kí*. In many cultures throughout the world we may discover this source has many names that represent the same idea.

The Spirit-self plays a viable part in enabling an individual to heal him- or herself once its role is understood and reified. The process that is used to connect one with his/her Spirit-self is meditation. Within a state of meditation we are able to communicate with the spirit world (an expressed dimension) and are able to receive what I call *Induced Knowledge*. Induced Knowledge, a term I use to represent spiritual knowledge given by a higher source, is another concept that appears frequently in this book. It is a pure representation of *knowing*.

Induced Knowledge can offer advanced knowledge of an event that will take place in the near future — a transference of knowledge given from a multidimensional source. This multidimensional source is sometimes referred to as a spirit guide, angel, guardian angel, multidimensional being, benevolent extraterrestrial, or other names depending on geographic location or culture.

I will periodically use the terms "Divine Source," "Source," "Creator/Creators," or "Great Spirit" to represent what is commonly referred to as "God." However, "God" is not identified as a monotheistic deity personality as promoted by theistic religions. Omni-benevolence expressing unconditional love and Divine Consciousness will be theoretically applied here to represent the term "God" throughout.

There are many reasons why you may be reading this book. You may be seeking answers to your own experiences with the paranormal and/or are pondering questions of life and of life after death. I can help you by sharing my life, but it is imperative for my reader to place all personal belief systems, including religious beliefs, on the backburner while you are exploring this book. I am not asking you to "believe" me, nor am I trying to persuade you in any manner. I am simply a witness to what I have experienced as my truth by way of radical empiricism (through one or more natural senses) and ask you only to think critically.

To think critically is not to approve or disapprove. It is an examination of evidence, assumptions, values, and reflection to evaluate credibility outside of one's prejudices, emotions, social ideologies, beliefs, and imposed stigmas. To be critical is to formulate solutions based on truth, as well as to be considerate to all involved. In essence one should be willing to evaluate one's self-deception and possible errors in accuracy, intellect, and logic, as well as self-serving biases. Basically, be open-minded without prejudice to reach your own conclusions.

The ideologies of my predecessors support the notion that self-discovery necessitates lifelong guidance of pastors, priest, mystics, sages, and *brujos* (warlocks) to "light" the path to enlightenment. You have no need for these individuals. Your inner voice will guide you to the truth that is already within you, expressed as feelings and experiences that bridge the communication between yourself and the Divinity via the Spirit-self. Moreover, you will not find spirituality in *this* book or *any* book you read — they will only serve as road signs. You will only find it... within you.

You will follow a progression of experiences I have had throughout my life and will find purpose behind those events. I will share how a highly evolved spirit guide has been directing me to these experiences so I may evolve spiritually — helping me reach a higher state of awareness.

My ultimate goal is to offer you the tools to find your own answers to your personal experiences. Furthermore, you will find within a new perspective of the mysteries about life and death.

This is my story. I share it with you to aid you in finding your spiritual bliss as a gift of love from me to all my *relations*, blood-related or not, who, in reading this book, choose to be part of my life. I come to you, my reader, as a stranger and leave a part of me with you, making us relatives in the profoundness of Divine Consciousness.

PART I

PSYCHOSPIRITUAL PSYCHOLOGY:

PATH OF PERSONAL DISCOVERY

Spirit Manifestation
First Glimpse of Light/The Awakening

"We are not human beings on a spiritual journey. We
are spiritual beings on a human journey."
STEPHEN COVEY

How is it possible for a deceased person to reappear in a physical form that represents his/her totality as if he/she had never died? How can a spirit take the form
of a functional body that breathes, talks, feels, and has all the characteristics of a
live three-dimensional human being? It is possible through a process called *Spirit
Manifestation*, a phenomenon where a spirit is able to manifest itself from the spirit
world to this dimension in order to take care of some form of "unfinished business."

The "unfinished business" can mean sending a message of love or a message of
comfort (e.g., letting family members know not to worry or grieve). There are other
times when this manifestation is undertaken to help a loved one in need. But what
I want to share with you is a profound encounter with Spirit Manifestation, which
in turn marked the beginning of a long quest to find answers to the questions I had
about the spirit world and its workings.

My father, Gilbert Z. Alaniz, was diagnosed with terminal cancer in the summer
of 1986 after complaining of lower back pain. His back pain spread to other areas
of his body — a cancer spreading throughout. My brother, Jerry, who is a physician,
met with my father's doctor, and together they announced to my family that my
father's cancer was incurable and he had approximately four months to live. I was
focused on my father's reaction when I heard this news and thought to myself, "I
am looking at a dead man." This may sound callous, but what I was telling myself

was every time from this point on when I see my father it would be as if he came back to life. This way, I was given opportunities to tell him how much I loved him and appreciated him being my father. Because of my experience as a combat veteran in Vietnam, I perceived death in a totally different manner than the average person.

My mother decided to keep my father at home where we could care for him, wanting to make him as comfortable as possible. I witnessed my father go from being able to walk normally to using a cane, then needing the support of a walker, to having to use a wheelchair, until he was ultimately confined to a bed. All of this transpired rapidly and within a four-month period.

One day, my father was in his wheelchair watching television with me in the family room, and he turned his head to his left toward the living room. There is a thoroughfare from the family room to the living room by which a person can approach the back area of my parents' house.

It seemed as though he recognized someone because he suddenly smiled, and his eyes widened. I looked through the large, open area expecting to see my mother or one of my brothers or sisters. Or perhaps it could be one of his close friends that visited him often. But there was no one standing there. My father was communicating with open space as he nodded his head in acknowledgment. I asked him who was there. He answered, "It's my grandmother."

"*Abuelita* Crusita?" I asked.

"Yes." *Abuelita* means "grandmother" in Spanish.

My great-grandmother, Cruz "Crusita" Alaniz, was especially close to my father, and all of her great-grandchildren adored her. She represented the epitome of love, and we all cherished her. She died at ninety-one years of age on September 25, 1970, when I was nineteen years old. I was curious and asked my father what his grandmother wanted. He answered me without turning his gaze from the direction of where she was: "She has come for me and Lawrence."

"What did you say?"

He repeated, "She has come for me and Lawrence." He nonchalantly turned his head back to the television program.

Lawrence Samora was my father's youngest brother, and at twenty-eight years of age also died of cancer after my father's passing. I knew that my father was under medication for pain but my intuition supported the idea that he had just experienced a visitation from my great-grandmother's spirit.

A month later my father was bedridden and my mother and I were in his room taking care of his daily needs. My mother was cleaning the room while I was spoon-feeding my father when again his attention was drawn away, this time toward the doorway leading into the hallway. I had a feeling that my father was having another visitation because I saw no one. I got my mother's attention so she could witness what was about to transpire. I asked my father, "Who is there?"

"It's my Grandmother Crusita."

"What does she want?"

He said, "She has come for me, Lawrence, and Richard."

Shocked I asked, "What! Are you sure?"

After he looked back toward *Abuelita* Crusita, my father offered a clarification: "She has come for me and Lawrence."

I was relieved to hear that, because I was the "Richard" he was referring to, and I was not ready to go with them to the spirit world — at least not yet. My great-grandmother held my father's attention for a few more seconds, and then he continued with his meal. I told my mother this happened once before, and perhaps my great-grandmother is my dad's guardian angel. Moreover, she would be there waiting for him and for Lawrence when they were ready to transition. I feel she was comforting my father and her visitations were meant to ease the experience of death so my father could make his transition to the spirit world easily and without fear.

This experience supports the idea that many have written about in countless articles and books. Someone will always be there for you as the moment of your transition draws closer, especially when you have an incurable sickness. It is usually the spirit of a family member who will visit you to bring you comfort and help ease the fear of death.

I have researched many stories where an individual who is sick and close to death will have visions of a deceased family member. A friend told me of one such story. While visiting his mother in the hospital, his mother told him to find a chair for his uncle to sit on while they were visiting with her. The mother did not know the uncle had passed away previously; they did not mention his death in order to save her any further trauma because of her fragile condition. They felt she was hallucinating when believing her brother was in the room visiting with the rest of the family. But in fact, they were the ones who could not see him. He came as a spirit, and she was the only person who was allowed to see him simply because he was there for her transition.

When my father finally passed on November 25, 1986, I carried out the tradition of cutting off my long hair. I tied an eagle feather to my ponytail with buckskin, placed it over his heart, and under his coat. Soon after we buried my father I rented out my home and moved my family in with my mother. I did not want her to be alone in such a large house that was full of my father's memories.

My wife and I occupied the master bedroom where my mother and father had previously slept, and my mother moved into one of the other bedrooms. It was two months after my father passed away when I had a life-changing experience that I feel was a gift of love and a major leap toward enhancing my knowledge of the spirit world.

It was an early morning when I was awakened by footsteps that resonated from the hardwood floor. I sat up on both elbows to see my father walking in from the hallway and approach the foot of my bed. The first words out of my mouth were, "Dad! I can't get over how good you look." When my father passed away he looked like an older shriveled man and was extremely underweight. The effects of cancer made a man of sixty-one look twice his age.

What surprised me was the notion that this spirit standing before me was my father. Instead of panicking I was amazed by how young and healthy he looked. He walked up to me, sat on my bed, and placed his right hand on my leg as he said, "How are you, *mijo* (son)?"

I knew this encounter was meant only for me, so I didn't wake up my wife to be a witness to what I was experiencing. I felt him touch me, and I felt the warmth and solidity of his hand as I touched him. I answered my father and told him I was doing well and I could not get over how good he looked.

What was really unusual was the fact that not only did he look healthy but he also looked younger. This experience was "my" evidence that in the spirit world we are young and healthy. After many years of research on spirits I found a significant number of reports expressing that spirits are at or around the age of thirty-five. That was it! My father was thirty-five, around my age at the time when I saw him as a manifested spirit. That is why I was amazed as to how great he looked; he was a young healthy man.

My father continued his conversation and said, "I have come to ask you to promise that you will take care of your mother for me."

I answered him with, "Hey. I'm here aren't I?"

He smiled then said, "I can see that, that's all I wanted to know. Take care of yourself." He got off of the bed and proceeded to leave.

I told him as he stood up, "Bye dad, I love you, take care of yourself." He smiled lovingly at me and left the room. He did not disappear into thin air — he just simply walked out — I stayed awake the rest of the morning.

I laid back and put my hands behind my head for support as I turned to look at my wife, thinking, "You are not going to believe this! You slept through a once-in-a-lifetime experience!" A sense of excitement came over me and I felt the purity of love. From that moment on I knew my life had changed.

Later my mother came into our room jumping with excitement as she said, "He was here! He was here! Your father was with me this morning!" This was confirmation that my experience was not only real but was supported by a simultaneous visit to my mother. She revealed to me that my father had appeared to her on another occasion. We both now have confirmation that there is life after death; and when we "die" we are healthy and are living in another dimension.

After this experience I pondered how it was scientifically possible for a spirit to manifest itself as a living person. If only science or the general public would also come to *know* that what had happened to my mother, me, and many others is proof of a spiritual world. Would people and science change their philosophies of life after death? I concluded, after much contemplation, that this knowledge is not meant for everyone. People will continue to "disbelieve" only because they fear the unknown and what is not written in their Holy Scriptures. I've yet to see any skeptics apply energy to enhance mankind; they waste it on debunking with weak evidence and *argumentum ad hominem* as their base argument.

What I experienced was real, and I am here to share with you this knowledge so you may perhaps understand your own experiences. The fact is we don't die; we transition to another dimension. In that dimension we are able to live as we did in this physical world and are able to create whatever we desire. I am your witness. Now it is up to you to be open to another reality and to live your life accordingly without the fear of death. You don't need to believe; you need to eradicate what many suffer from — the fear of death.

Everyone is destined to find his or her own way to spirituality either in this lifetime or another. We all have the ability to experience a separate reality when it comes to spirituality and understanding the meaning of "God" within our life according to our visions or lack thereof. Perhaps the only way to get back on track is to really listen and hear your spirit guide's constant conversation that he/she is having with you internally in the name of love and God consciousness.

Many skeptics and religious zealots have questioned and continue to question my experiences, which is fair. I was in conversation with an elderly gentleman, a pastor, who is a born-again Christian and who described himself as a "God-fearing" person of strong faith. When I shared my experience about my father appearing to me, his response was it was not my father. Rather, it was Satan who manifested as my father in order to fool me. He explained, "Satan is very powerful, and only Jesus is capable of rising from the dead. Only those who are born again will rise with the second coming of Jesus Christ when he will resurrect only the believers and the faithful." According to him it was impossible that it could have been my father. "If it is not in the Bible, then it is from Satan." He was stating an absolute according to his logic simply because he "believes." I remember thinking, "If it was Satan, then he screwed up." It was an act of love that brought my father to me that day. How could Satan appear in a state of love? The elder *believes* in what he reads, I *know* what I experienced. It's that simple.

This Christian is abiding by fear, and Satan rules his world because he gives energy to evil. He *believes* Satan acts as a co-benefactor given to humans by God. Furthermore, Satan has the power to override a person's love, and if we don't abide by the church's teachings, God will be angry and will punish us — sounds like fear to me.

We will all experience spiritual consciousness either in this life or in the next life. How we attach ourselves to our current beliefs will be a condition of our reaching a spiritual awakening.

Another example of fear created by *belief* is the time I attended a birthday party with my musician friends. While I was listening to my friend's brother's Christian band play I was amazed by their talent. Suddenly I heard my silent voice tell me I would be playing with this band. I thought it impossible because I had been a retired musician for over thirteen years. I gave up music to master the martial arts long ago. My music equipment was long in storage, and after ending a twenty-year musical career, I did not want to play music any longer. There had to be a special reason why I was to play with this group.

After they played their last set, I approached the lead singer, who was also the bass player. I conveyed to him how much I appreciated his musical ability as a bass player since I was one also. He waved over the lead guitarist, and they expressed to me they were looking for a bass player to relieve the singer so he could concentrate more on vocals. The drummer whom I knew told them I was the musician he was talking about earlier.

They asked me to audition. I told them I had not played the bass in over thirteen years and I was very rusty. However, I accepted their offer, explaining I had received Induced Knowledge that I would play with them. I'm more than sure they didn't know what I meant by Induced Knowledge — I explained later.

I was given a tape of their music to learn for the audition, and a few weeks later I performed for them — they were impressed. I made them an offer. I would rehearse with them for four weeks and at the end of the fourth week we each could decide if I would continue to play with them. At the end of the allotted time we had a meeting. They wanted me to stay, and I accepted.

Now that I was officially in the band I was compelled to make a statement. I said, "This band no longer belongs to you, it belongs to God, and when you come here to practice your egos are to be left outside the door." They all agreed. I feel my spirit guide urged me to say these words for a reason unknown at the time. But I knew it was Induced Knowledge. It is amazing to think that I was not a Christian and I had long ago decided never to play music again professionally, yet here I was playing in a Christian rock band!

I realized later the reason for joining this band was not to revive my music career. After a few more weeks of rehearsal we had a conversation concerning my spirituality. I shared my experiences, focusing on the visitation of my father after his passing. Like the elderly gentleman I mentioned earlier, they told me it was Satan not my father. Their view was I was dealing with demons, which caused them concern. The lead singer, who was an assistant pastor at their church, said I probably had the gift of discernment.

The following week the lead guitarist who had recently become a student of mine in martial arts phoned me and said the group nominated him to tell me they wanted to go back to a four-piece band. At that very moment I received Induced Knowledge that they had decided I no longer was welcome in the band because they were afraid of what I had shared with them earlier — and that the decision had nothing to do with my musical ability. I mentioned to him I was fine with it and I was glad to have had the opportunity to meet new friends. I wished them success, and he expressed that he wanted to continue his training with me. I agreed and was looking forward to maintaining a friendship.

Two weeks later, after our martial arts class, I asked him if the reason I was asked to leave the band was due to my spiritual experiences. He answered, "Yes." I thanked him for his honesty. He said they couldn't figure out why God had brought me to them. The drummer knew I was part Native American and felt I was probably practicing witchcraft. The guitar player added he tried to tell them I was not evil, that he had spent time training with me, was in my home and never sensed anything evil about me. But their spiritual ignorance and fear overcame them.

I told him I knew why God brought me to them. I said, "I knew you were not right with 'God' and with the doctrine of your religion. God, or more likely your spirit guides, brought me to this band to give you knowledge, to teach you about ego and to expose your faith." He admitted he and the assistant pastor were having issues with their faith. I asked him, "What if God brought me to you guys to save me? If you are Christians, then isn't that one way you are to serve God? If I was evil, then as Christians, you have an obligation to bring God's love to me and not cast me aside." He admitted they thought about that possibility — but they didn't want to take a chance — they were living in fear.

The band broke up a few weeks later; the reason was a power struggle of egos over the band's musical direction. I am sure they will continue to live in fear, maybe "backslide" every now and then as they praise the word of Jesus through their music.

When it comes to Spirit Manifestation we can't only *believe* what has been given to us in scriptures and label the unknown as evil. We have to examine our own experiences and those of others to gain knowledge of a greater reality. My choice is to *know* by my experiences and to research the claims of others to find further support for what I have come to know as truth, especially when it is manifested through love.

The Five Ways of Knowing
Exploring Perception and Interpretation

"Do not believe in anything simply because you have heard it. Do not believe in anything simply because it is spoken and rumored by many. Do not believe in anything simply because it is found written in your religious books. Do not believe in anything merely on the authority of your teachers and elders. Do not believe in traditions because they have been handed down for many generations. But after observation and analysis, when you find that anything agrees with reason and is conducive to the good and benefit of one and all, then accept it and live up to it."

BUDDHA

Most of what people *believe* is due to either a constructed belief system or faith in an ideology as a product of truth. To help you understand my perspective, let's take a look at *The Five Ways of Knowing*, to examine how a person develops a belief system through a process that involves from one to a combination of five specific ways.

According to Vernon Padgett, PhD, *The Five Ways of Knowing* was developed by Lyle Creamer, PhD, during his professorship at California State University, Long Beach. He argues that one or a combination of the five ways are basically how our society comes to know things to be true by way of tenacity, intuition, authority, reason or rationalism, and empiricism (science).

Professor Creamer explains how belief systems are supported by one or more of these five specific areas to formulate how societies come to accept something as a representation of truth. I will briefly identify each of the five areas that were given to me in 2004 by Dr. Padgett, a research methods professor at Rio Hondo College in Southern California. I will follow up with my perspective to demonstrate how these socially accepted ideas about *believing* can at times be critical in how we think and can create errors in determining a truth. Belief systems for the most part are culturally specific and are passed down to generations as an accepted means of truth.

The Five Ways of Knowing
By Professor Lyle Creamer

1. Tenacity: We have always done it this way.
2. Intuition: It just feels right in my heart, or gut.
   Example: Men are better drivers than women. Why? It just feels right to me, in my heart (even though it may be wrong!).
3. Authority: Getting information from others whom we respect and trust.
4. Reason or Rationalism: They are different, but both stress the outcome of reasoning, which produces knowledge that is superior to other ways of acquiring knowledge.
5. Empiricism (Science): Direct sensory or perceptual experience; the only self-correcting system of attaining knowledge, free from errors of others.

I will express how societies have used one or more of these five ways to support possible *errors* in their thinking. I will argue that in some situations when one justifies his/her beliefs in such a manner it can be problematic when one wishes to support his/her perspective of truth. Truth to some is a set of ideas that allow them to verify their own beliefs to meet their needs sufficiently and expediently. However, fidelity to one's beliefs in most cases defiles truth.

1. Tenacity — "*We have always done it this way.*" Our parents and their parents believe it to be true. To refute this I could say that our parents could have been wrong all this time, but yet we will continue to think as they did and believe according to what was handed down generation after generation. Even if we are wrong we will feel comfortable in continuing to support our belief systems. Tenacity simply implies, "If it was good enough for our parents and grandparents, it is good enough for us."

2. Intuition (not a spiritual psychic intuition) — "*It just feels right in my heart or gut.*" For example: "Men are better drivers than women. Why? Because it just feels right to me in my heart." Even though it may be possibly wrong and untrue, one will continue to support this belief with potential prejudices. Our society can even support this gut feeling with a scientific study (empiricism) formulated around the hypothesis that men are better drivers than women. All that is needed are a few *male* scientists who are performing the study in gathering data for a hypothesis that supports that males are better drivers. We can also have *female* scientists perform a similar study that supports a hypothesis that women are better drivers. Both of these findings can be published because the data has been gathered using the scientific method. As one can see, the tools of science, if manipulated, may be considered subjective when the scientists focus on data that will support what THEY consciously want and ignore data that may refute or not support their hypothesis with significant statistics.

In this next scenario, a null hypothesis is a default statement made by either the male or female research team with a new twist, "men and women are equally good drivers." The null hypothesis is presumed true until it is statistically proven otherwise. If the null hypothesis is rejected — found not to be true — it supports "there is a difference" between male and female drivers. It does not state which group are better drivers, but rather that they are different.

Once any of these two research teams can produce data that states they are unequal they can manipulate the alternate hypothesis if they choose to do so with statistical analysis to support the hypothesis favoring men or women being the better drivers. Although the researcher is supposed to be non-biased, the male or female research team can produce data to support what they or their employer favors (either for political or social reasons) if they wish to do so by omitting data that can manipulate statistical results. Of course society is a benefactor of science; however, it is not a perfect system especially in explaining human behavior.

3. Authority (This is the most dangerous.) — *"Getting information from others whom we respect and trust."* For example, "There are weapons of mass destruction held by an axis of evil." The majority followed the Bush administration's agenda after the September 11th attack in 2001 simply because we as a society have been conditioned to believe that a person in the highest authority would always tell the public the truth. Have we never been lied to by our politicians, lawyers, institutions, priests, cult leaders, heads of corporations, and parents? Fear of a "mushroom cloud" was used to gain support for war.

4. Reason or Rationalism (Logic may be in this category.) — *"They are different, but both stress the outcome of reasoning that produces knowledge that is superior to other ways of acquiring knowledge."* One may be able to reason with the knowledge one has. However, what if the knowledge is limited and incomplete? One may not have all the facts or information and the issues of multicultural perspectives are not usually taken into consideration when one reasons. For example: According to Professor

Mike Connor, PhD, historically the literature states that Native American fathers were considered to have poor fathering skills compared to turn-of-the-century Anglo-American fathers. It's no wonder, as standards of fathering were based in Eurocentric ideology. Anglo-American fathers at that time were disciplinarians, authoritarians, and were not nurturing since nurturing was viewed as a mother's responsibility. In contrast, Native American fathers were nurturing and rarely disciplined their children. Culturally, Native Americans allowed their children to learn by interaction and modeling after the behavior of tribal members. Generative fathering was a practice in indigenous matriarchal societies, meaning that uncles, grandfathers, or extended relatives played a crucial role in the upbringing and nurturing of their children. This contradicts historical paradigms of Eurocentric fathering. Therefore in this case, the premise that Native Americans practice poor fathering skills as a reasonable and rational idea is a false statement.

5. Empiricism (Science) – *"A direct sensory or perceptual experience. The only self-correction system of attaining knowledge that is free from the errors of others."* This is believed to be objective observation but, in some cases, it is subjective. Historically the world was flat and it was reasonable to think it as such. However, new information led science to change its mind and produce a new theory, that the world is actually round. The greatest asset of science is its capacity to improve research methods. But we do not take into consideration, because we can't prove it with science and technology at this time, that there are multidimensional forces. Science shuns experiences that take place outside of our given reality. People all over the world have paranormal experiences through *radical empiricism* yet science will not accept the idea that there is something beyond what our current technology can process. Therefore, this prejudice limits the progression of behavioral science. Scientists decide what facts are acceptable; people who challenge their authority are considered to suffer from hallucinations and delusional thoughts.

I can certainly try to argue each of my points pertaining to these five ways of knowing. But there is only one sure way of knowing and that is to know through personal experience. Knowing by experience is the truest form of a reality perspective. Albeit there are some limitations to personal experience, but nonetheless it is far more reliable than trusting or having faith in something or someone merely because we read about it or heard about it.

Knowing is a process that is beyond cognitive reasoning or logic. It is an innate sensory feeling, devoid of belief and faith, and is subjective. It is materialistic in that one is in a state of experiencing due to sensory perception. For example, you "know" that some person has just walked into your room. You know this because you are experiencing it with sensory perception as you *see* the individual enter your room. You heard the person when he/she greeted you, and you physically felt the person while shaking hands or hugging him/her. There is no need for belief or even to turn to faith that you experienced the person enter your room.

To extend the concept of knowing, let me offer a twist. Say the person who walked into your room, John, had died in a car accident a few months earlier. Now we can ask this question: If you are experiencing John walking into your room, does that mean you are having a hallucination? Psychologists (behavioral scientists) will argue "yes," you are experiencing one of many forms of hallucinations. The psychologist's "Bible," *Diagnostic and Statistical Manual of Mental Disorders (DSM-IV-TR)*, will categorize human behavior within the scientific nature of psychology, omitting any consideration or concept of the supernatural or what William James refers to as "transempirical entities."

Let us gather some facts. You saw, touched, and talked to John, were awake during daylight hours, and are considered to have a sound mind. You had an experience of your own involving *radical empiricism*. However, according to the standard scientific method (DSM-IV-TR), you would have been *thought to have* been hallucinating. Therefore, because science has not reached a level of mysticism or multidimensional knowledge, and is stuck in a conventional state of knowledge (i.e., the world is flat), we as a society will not give credence or authority to the person who is having the experience. This is the basis of my assertion that human behavioral science, in some cases, is guilty of subscribing to an "innocent ignorance" when directed toward paranormal events or mysticism.

Most people represent *belief* as if it is a knowing of truth. But in reality belief is something you read about or what someone told you. Faith has no need for intellectual debate. There is no need to *know*, and faith is supported with belief.

My wish is not to offend my readers by placing absolute limitations on belief systems and faith, but to merely give a different perspective. It is important to respect the ideologies of others, especially in their religious faith. However, I am arguing there is a considerable difference between *believing* and *knowing*, which is important if one wants to reach a higher level of truth and spiritual consciousness.

There are no absolutes when it comes to truth for it is always evolving. However, there are limitations to our growth when one adheres to ideologies based on a belief without realizing there is nothing more inevitable than change. It is perfectly acceptable to have a passion for one's belief. However, it is important to be open to a greater experience. We must all reach out to explore the possibilities that our beliefs can be enhanced to a greater truth. This is possible if we push ourselves to achieve knowledge outside of our belief systems.

When I am asked how do I know something is true, I am secure in answering, "I simply know because I have experienced it for myself." I don't need to believe; I know through my experience, which is void of any preconceived ideologies or prejudices.

THREE

Induced Knowledge

How the Wisdom Arrives/Training the Brain to Recognize Wisdom

> "Knowing others is intelligence; Knowing thyself is true wisdom.
> Mastering others is strength; Mastering yourself is true power."
>
> SUN TZU

There are spiritual gifts mentioned in the Bible, and one of these is *knowledge*. We access knowledge in order to help or guide ourselves within the process of life experiences to reach a higher level of spiritual consciousness. When a person experiences Induced Knowledge one has the feeling of knowing something without knowing how or by what means that knowledge was manifested. One just simply knows something is or will be. Induced Knowledge is an experience that once developed can be used as a tool for spiritual growth. This is not only for your own growth, but also to help guide others away from an undesired experience or toward a positive life process.

Within this knowledge there is no need for a belief system. One will know by experience that Induced Knowledge is purposeful and will guide one within the experience. It is void of doubt, and there is no need to "believe" what you have experienced. It is pure knowledge that was induced by your spirit guide.

A *belief system* on the other hand is a comprehensive set of values or rules developed by a dominant class of individuals. It is organized, repeated, instilled within a population, and is eventually accepted as truth. The belief system, composed of a set of rules, usually guides using symbols and traditions. It is not necessary to prove or offer experience that testifies to the veracity of a belief; rather, beliefs are simply accepted and are at times a condition of faith. If these sets of rules are solid, they become an impediment to accepting ideas outside of the belief.

To *believe* is to trust with faith, and faith is supported with a belief. It must be noted that within belief there is a shadow of a doubt. Let us examine this further. If you stand on a table and fall backward thinking I will catch you, you are operating under the belief that I will allow no injury to you. Even though you "believe" I will catch you, mentally your confirmation will be when you "feel" my arms securing your fall. Until you "feel" my arms you are harboring a shadow of a doubt. As you believe, you are also thinking I may not be strong enough, quick enough, or my attention may be sidetracked. Having "faith" that you will be caught is simply falling backward without discrimination or reservation — you are not waiting to feel my arms secure your fall. This is known as *blind faith*. Knowing you will be caught is having experienced being caught by me before. You "know" it is possible — no need to believe and there is no doubt.

Once one has developed a viable meditation practice and accepts the purpose of Induced Knowledge, one can identify its manifestation and can recognize its intent. It is a silent voice within which guides you, perhaps a telepathic means of communication between you and your spirit guide. It is not an actual voice, but rather your inner voice that communicates a message. This voice is not necessarily audible; we can think of it as more of a thought or *feeling* rather than hearing a personal dialog within you. This feeling of communication is so vivid, that once developed, an individual can tell the difference between having a mental conversation with oneself and being directed by one's spirit guide.

Some people may label this type of experience as a "premonition" or "gut feeling," which usually involves a logical explanation to make sense of the experience. In other words, it just came and then it left. It is accepted "as is" without any prominent reasoning behind the feeling. Usually they will not take it seriously and will categorize the experience as a coincidence. When one comes to understand it is communication from the spirit world to serve us, then one will no longer need to use "logical" explanations. One will learn to accept and acknowledge the message and proceed with the information given with sincerity. He/she is then connected to and is in acceptance of his/her spirit guide.

Induced Knowledge is designed to inform so we may relate to the information and change what needs to be changed in order to serve our best and highest good.

Induced Knowledge can prevent negative experience if we take the proper action by following the guidance. Once one develops the ability to recognize this knowledge and is able to detect the difference between internal thought dialog and Induced Knowledge, one is able to make a difference in one's life experiences.

Induced Knowledge has served me well. This following story is an example of how Induced Knowledge can serve another person.

I received Induced Knowledge that my friend's father was going to be diagnosed with cancer and given an unfavorable prognosis. I also learned the same friend would never bear any children. I knew the purpose of the Induced Knowledge, so I phoned her to give her the message. She did not respond positively when I mentioned, "I have a message for you," because she simply did not *believe* in my abilities. I told her once before of something that was going to happen to her — and it did — but she felt it was a coincidence. She refused to accept I was able to conceive any knowledge beyond something that was coincidental.

It was revealed to me to refrain from pushing the concept of Induced Knowledge to anyone unless he/she is open to it. Therefore, I just left things as they were and allowed her to learn in her own time. As it turned out, at a later date she told me her father was sick, and they were desperate to find him the proper medical care. The doctor her father was seeing did not diagnose cancer until it was too late — it was incurable.

During the time her father was dying of cancer, my friend called to tell me she was pregnant. I could not help but hope I was wrong about her infertility. However, in the same breath she said she was having an abortion. I asked her to consider alternatives to the abortion, but she insisted that was what she was going to do. She was not ready to have a child, even though she was in love with her boyfriend. She had the abortion a few days later, and her father eventually passed away. Now that she is married, and ready to start a family, she is unable to get pregnant — I feel she lost her only chance at having a child.

The reason I receive Induced Knowledge is not only to help others with the information given to me, but also to educate those who are interested in learning more about the unknown. My interaction with other people who have had similar experiences also gives support and confirmation to the possibilities of multidimensional communication and the existence of the spirit world.

During my years of practice as a spiritual counselor I received information through Induced Knowledge that has helped me to gain insight into the basis of my clients' problems. I have also been guided as to what proper direction should be used to help in their healing process, which I know came from my spirit guide. This is an integral part of my system for helping individuals with emotional issues.

Most of the knowledge that I am calling upon in writing this book is Induced Knowledge, which has allowed me to understand how the spirit world works, along with my various experiences with spirit entities. I feel these experiences — and what I have learned from them — have helped me facilitate a program that I offer people who are willing and ready to move toward spiritual consciousness.

I have been told so many times by people that if God would give them concrete evidence of the existence of the spirit world they would change their beliefs. My answer is, "You will never believe what you see and will question the experience with your logical mind because of your preconceived beliefs. Your fear will over-power the truth because you cannot fathom the idea. And most of all you will be afraid that people will think less of you."

If "God" would reveal Himself, no one would believe it was really God because everyone has his or her different opinions as to what God is or looks like. The masses would probably try to kill Him. Historically, the killing of prophets is not new to many societies. And people would debate if they had just killed God or a representation of Satan. If extraterrestrials (ETs) appear to us and say they created us in their image (there are reports of humanoid ETs) the masses would not accept this. The popular concept of God as the sole creator of all things would override all other ideas of creation.

Most believe God only talked to righteous men thousands of years ago and any recent profound communications from God are evil or sacrilegious. Perhaps Induced Knowledge would be viewed by religious zealots as communication from Satan. I feel there is constant communication from the spirit world throughout time by means of Induced Knowledge as well as other ways.

Trying to explain the unlimited essence of what "God" is, without using a noun or pronoun to people who already have a preconceived notion, is like trying to explain to a fish what water is. Fish don't see water and perhaps don't understand it; because they take it for granted, they have no other concept to compare it with. If you are in the ocean and try to grab a handful of water, you can't, because you are in it — it is grabbing you. A fish swims in water and that's all it has ever known until you take it out, and when it dies it will understand its relationship to water.

Like the fish, do we have to die in order to understand who and what God really is? If it is important to know the truth, you will have to reach a spiritual awakening, or transition to the spirit world (die). In my perspective, it does not matter what God is in terms of shape, form, or tangibility. The word "God" is limiting; I can go on and on without being able to define what God is, and that is why words are the least valuable form of communicating an idea. I have experienced telepathic thought and feelings, and find they are more useful in expressing a concept.

It is within the relationship we have with the Source or Creator for guidance that is important for us in order to heal and evolve spiritually. I don't need God to be a he, she, or even an energy force for me to understand the unconditional love that defines God. It's not really important for God to be majestic in a long flowing robe with white hair, a long beard, and a deep penetrating voice that represents authority.

Sometimes I wonder if Jesus was a short, dark-skinned, balding, chubby, unattractive man instead of the handsome, tall, white-skinned, blue-eyed Jesus who is identified in all the paintings that depict him. Would people think differently of Jesus because of his appearance and still value his teachings? We are conditioned to believe what makes us feel good, and if representing Jesus as a handsome prophet makes us feel better, then that is what you will be given. I prefer the truth, and regardless what the truth may be, as long as I am in the midst of unconditional love, I will feel the goodness within me and all around me.

Each person has the ability to find truth if you are not a slave to controlling factors from others. It is necessary for all citizens to follow the laws of the land only if they benefit equally and with fairness. However, control by an elite faction of any society benefits only the small percentage of those who are in control. The *truth*, as I have mentioned before, is within all of us. We merely have to remember.

Many cultures have at their basis a fundamental belief system that at times can undermine the need to experience outside ideas. Belief will discourage one to question. This is dangerous to any person or society that seeks truth. Again I will stress the fact that we learned to accept and follow what was given to us by previous generations.

There is a growing need to break away from tenacious ideologies. Look around, and you will find pockets of individuals within your social network who are starting to express a desire for or openness to other ideas of spirituality outside of religious doctrine. People have more resources they can go to for information.

Famous people are sharing their stories on various television programs having to do with the paranormal. Most confess they have changed their views because of their experiences that brought them to a new understanding outside of what they formerly supported. While some are fearful of a paranormal event, others express how they have become more aware of spirituality having had a positive paranormal experience that is void of fear. It is beyond their religious beliefs — instead it is a valid experience that holds the truth for them.

I feel there is nothing better than direct communication from one's spirit guide through Induced Knowledge, and it is an important foundation for this book in order to understand how I perceive my experiences. My education is in psychology, which allows me to understand human cognition and behavior to express how your beliefs are affected by five basic concepts, presented in Chapter Two, describing how *you* come to know something as a representation of truth.

Perhaps you will identify with some of my experiences. Perhaps you will support and confirm what you already know and learn to accept it without fear of being stigmatized. You will find I do not live by fear; I am on a path to awareness that is void of belief systems and am unequivocally guided by Induced Knowledge.

Pyschospiritual Psychology
Introduction to an Applied Theory

Upon the inception of academic studies, human behavior was categorized as a philosophy by Ancient Greek and Ancient Egyptian scholars who diligently studied the many components of the mind and human behavior. Psychology didn't gain its independence as a scientific discipline until the 1870s. However, today many view psychology as a pseudoscience.

Historically, many cultures have developed various theories to hypothesize the nature of the mind, soul, and spirit as a function of human spirituality. Superstitious cultures used incantations and other processes as remedies to heal diseases believed to be caused by demons and other supernatural forces.

In Ancient Asia, psychological experiments studied the diseases of the mind. Within India's ancient Vedanta scriptures the theory of "the self" identified self-realization. Hallucinations, nightmares, dementia, epilepsy, vertigo, and other conditions were phenomena studied by many cultures that viewed these ailments as an imbalance of mind, body, and spirit.

Modern psychology was founded by German and American psychologists who developing theories and applied methods of psychoanalysis, hypnosis, interpretation of the conscious and unconscious mind, as well as other notable areas that have influenced Western culture.

As psychology evolved, behavioral psychology eliminated all aspects of the spirit, which were seen as archaic and superstitious. Eventually, the focus was on "Nature vs. Nurture" as a means to identify the influence of human behavior stemming from one's genetics or environment, respectively.

It is my feeling that the future of psychology will come full circle and eventually accept the "Nature, Nurture, and Spirit" theory, which includes spirit consciousness as a product of the human experience. In today's study of human psychology we find a few psychologists who are drawn to transpersonal psychology and parapsychology, which are outside the realm of the conservative scientific community. Researchers who study hypnosis and other means for evaluating paranormal events are presenting their findings to mainstream science using the scientific method.

Dr. Michael Newton, a psychologist who previously worked on behavioral modification, found similarities reported by his patients as he was gathering data using hypnosis. Initially a skeptic grounded in science, Dr. Newton experienced a revelation about the possibilities stemming from past-life regression. After many years of research his data found similar descriptions and experiences reported by his clients when under hypnosis as they described their own prior death and existence in a previous life.

Transpersonal psychology (TP) integrates psychological theories and methods of spiritual disciplines. Through research and experience, TP evaluates methods for developing one's human potential and realization. Noted for inspiring modern studies in psychology and mysticism, William James, Carl Jung, and Abraham Maslow, as well as others, have been influential in furthering the research of self-development, transcendent states of consciousness, and spiritual concepts affecting human psychology.

Sofia University (formerly The Institute of Transpersonal Psychology), an accredited school established in 1975, presents TP as an academic discipline and not a spiritual movement. The school offers a path to earn a degree in transpersonal psychology with postgraduate courses in counseling and clinical psychology. The SU website states, "Transpersonal psychologists work across disciplines and draw on insights from not only the various areas of psychology, but also the sciences of cognition, consciousness, and the paranormal; philosophy; social and cultural theory; integral health theories and practices; poetry, literature, and the arts; and, the world's spiritual and wisdom traditions." (*http://www.sofia.edu/about/transpersonal.php*)

After twenty-five years of studying various indigenous spiritual healing practices and modern psychological theories, I found a significant number of people who were seeing therapists for many years and not getting any results. By interviewing those who were willing to share their attitudes and personal experiences with therapy, I realized that even though it made them feel good for a relatively short period to have someone to talk to about life issues, they were not getting well. They resigned themselves to just "living with it."

After studying many areas of modern psychology, I felt that in some cases the inclusion of my mixed theory of shamanic practice and modern psychological theory could be helpful for those not benefiting from standard therapeutic practices. This was my motivation in developing a new model as a cross-disciplinary approach to psychological and psycho-physiological healing within my practice as a spiritual counselor. I call this new paradigm "Psychospiritual Psychology."

Within this model it was important to redefine spirituality as it is viewed today by various religions. According to the Psychospiritual model, spirituality is twofold. It is a transitional awareness of the Spirit-self as a continuum consciousness foremost. Secondly, spirituality in its most viable form represents a multidimensional state of inspiration directing the will of the individual to evolve to a positive manifestation of self-love and unconditional love for humanity to promote human dignity. Guidance received from this multidimensional realm is either from one or more multidimensional entities that are not defined as absolute or without limitations, but are represented as, and not limited to, spirit guides, co-creators, guardian angels, or Creator/Creators, all being representations of God Consciousness.

The focus of Psychospiritual Psychology is to connect the individual's personality to the Spirit-self and to use this knowledge as a spiritual support system for individuals suffering from maladaptive behavioral disorders, bringing about positive emotional, behavioral, developmental, physiological, and psychological well-being. Furthermore, the Psychospiritual model promotes awareness of differentiating factors in healing to include multicultural belief systems. Without parameters, it must and will always evolve.

Spirituality is an extension of the inner being's connection to what the conscious mind longs for, to seek a higher awareness, and for "self-actualization" (realization of one's full potential), a term used by psychologist Abraham Maslow. To live in one's potential is to experience outside of what we have been coerced to believe in within our four-dimensional world and mindset. Moreover, it is imperative to live in the present moment without fixative past or future influences. This idea must be approached fearlessly.

The influence of doctrines and belief systems can only keep one in the realm of tenacious social and cultural parameters. They do not allow one to progress beyond rules and ideologies formulated by a belief system.

Everything that we seek is within the present moment, the "here and now" as conveyed in Gestalt therapy. It is within the silent mind that is not influenced by the active mind that one can process awareness through meditation. With much practice of meditation anyone can experience a heightened state of observation all the while trying to avoid mental gymnastics — this is the key to its purpose. When you are in the "here and now," you are deep within the self — the Spirit-self. Within this internal consciousness, one is in the moment, free from external static and able to communicate using a different intelligence. When one is in a meditative state it is possible to commune with a multidimensional source.

The problem most people have with meditation lies in expectations, which promote a busy mind. This is the opposite of what meditation really offers. The goal is not to silence the mind completely; the goal is to simply observe without prejudice and to eliminate the influence of the personality, which constantly needs to *understand*. To attempt to understand is fuel for the busy mind. Awareness is a state of being in the moment with no past and no future, no space and no time, no entry and no exit.

Two primary tools that are promoted within Psychospiritual Psychology are awareness of active multidimensional forces and the benefits of meditation for awareness. One goal is to reject the limitations that conservative social ideology demands for you to continue to believe in, meaning you are unstable if you believe in anything that is outside of what is acceptable in our society. Social structures are tenacious in setting rules and boundaries for what is normal.

Any individual can change his/her life simply by learning to see life from a different perspective — from within. Learning to categorize one's thoughts and behavior as either being based on love or fear, one can learn to manifest a more positive outlook on life. The ultimate goal is to have unconditional love for yourself first, and then for others. However, it does not mean you have to keep negative people in your circle.

You will be faced with negativity constantly in your life and in various forms; therefore, it is important to circumvent negativity when possible and most of all to not give energy to it. Acceptance is a major key in facing past and unavoidable future negative experiences. It is also most important to learn to move forward with a positive attitude and accept that all things are for a reason. How you deal with adversities will factor in how you are affected, but the final emotion should be to stay in a constant state of joy, free of negativity and fear.

I will offer here a brief description of the basic principles of Psychospiritual Psychology and how it can be used by the professional therapist who is open to a holistic approach to therapy as well as individuals who are ready to move toward a self-help process in therapy. However, it is important to understand the psychological theories of Gestalt and psychodrama therapy, and *Balík* Meditation, which incorporates *Chí* channeling as a dynamic breathing meditative practice.

It is of utmost importance for the client to be free from any belief systems. In order to move forward one must relinquish former attitudes in thinking — after all, one's current thinking is what put him/her in his/her current state of mind. Next is for the client to establish affirmations as to what he/she wishes to accomplish, which sets a mental and spiritual goal — there is a light at the end of the tunnel, even though I can't see it, I can feel it.

A secondary but crucial aspect of Psychospiritual Psychology is the separation of the self using a synthesis of Gestalt and psychodrama therapy as a technique to split the personality into two parts, each expressing its perspectives and concerns. For example, Sarah is torn between wanting independence from a controlling mother, and understanding her mother's need to control her. Each part of Sarah will be represented in a separate chair facing one another and she will have a discussion to defend each view, perhaps argue and express underlying emotions, and eventually compromise. Once the deep-rooted issue surfaces as a result of the discussion, a contract between both personalities is established thereby creating an acceptance for the good of the whole.

Once the underlying issue is identified, the participant can have communion with his/her spirit guide during the practice of meditation, first acknowledging the spirit guide, and second asking for guidance. My forthcoming book, *Balík Meditation — Wellness to Mind-Body-Spirit*, offers readers a systematic approach to meditation as a tool to connect to their Spirit-selves and communicate with their spirit guides.

The idea is not to have the participant "believe" in spirit guides or anything during the process — the worst thing is to offer another belief system. The goal is for the participant to have an actual experience so he/she may "know" through experience the existence of a greater source, which he/she may address as a spirit guide or guardian angel. Eventually he/she will have an "ah-ha" moment if done correctly and if the right attitude is present from both the therapist and the client/participant.

When everything is in alignment the door to the spirit realm is opened and all things are possible. The therapist who also practices meditation will find he/she is being guided with Induced Knowledge, which offers valuable information about the participant that was not previously known. In this process, each person's spirit guide is working in tandem to bring about a spiritual healing for the participant. Using this method I have helped people with much success. One of my clients was under medication while seeing a therapist in weekly sessions for over two years. However, after three months learning and practicing *Balík* Meditation and *Balík* Yoga, along with counseling sessions with me, my client was able to have control over her issues, and in turn over her life. Anyone can learn my meditation method by studying with a qualified *Balík* meditation instructor or by reading my forthcoming book *Balík Meditation.*

This process has nothing to do with miracles; it is about the participant finding his/her own way to bring about a healing. I simply guide them to the door; they have to knock, and then accept what is on the other side as they enter fearlessly. It's really that simple.

Will this technique/theory work on everyone even with deep psychological issues such as schizophrenia? I have never had a client with this type of condition so I don't know, but I am close to a few people who have a family member who is schizophrenic, and feel psychoactive drugs and other approaches to therapy are necessary in those cases. My success has been in helping my clients with depression, low self-esteem, anxiety disorders, bereavement, and dissociative identity disorder (multiple personalities). I feel both science and shamanism are valuable approaches to providing treatment for the vast amount of differentiation within the myriad of psycho-physiological illnesses and psychological disorders. With time I feel there will be a breakthrough in this holistic approach to mental wellness.

PART II

KARMONIC EXPERIENCE:

PERSONAL LIFE PLAN FOR SPIRITUAL CONSCIOUSNESS

Karmonic Experience
Life Plan Guided by Divine Intervention

"To discuss the problems connected with the stages of human
development is an exacting task, for it means nothing less than unfolding
a picture of psychic life in its entirety from the cradle to the grave."
CARL JUNG, *MODERN MAN IN SEARCH OF A SOUL*

The human experience is motivated by life challenges, and these challenges create a desire to find meaning that is essential to our existence. Within each and every experience is a defined reality. When there is a profound turn in that process, either good or bad, and it presents an indispensable teaching or awareness, I consider it a Divine Intervention. This intervention is from a higher source, and not of this space-time dimension. It is designed to effect a higher consciousness relative to the experience in order to plant a seed that God or the spiritual realm is involved. The Divinity, either directly or indirectly, is acting upon the experience to induce spirit consciousness directed toward one's "Karmonic Experience."

Miracles either small or large, that interrupt the scientific laws of nature and have beneficial properties, are actions or influences of God, spirit guides, or guardian angels, and are considered acts of Divine Intervention. Moreover, a miracle that is unlikely statistically or not identified as a fortuitous event is a phenomenon that may be evidence for supernatural beings interacting with humans.

In the Buddhist teachings, the law of karma is the follow-up action from a previous event or action. Karma is an action, thought, or what one says especially when it has intention. This intention, positive or negative, will process itself in this lifetime or in the next lifetime, creating a cycle of rebirth. Karma can also be understood as cause and effect, but to simplify karma, we can say "what goes around comes around."

If an event was causal by a previous-lifetime contributory event, then that event may be subject to how or what the individual will experience in yet another lifetime. This may provoke a process called *Samsara* — a round of death and rebirth — a cycle of incarnation — in other words reincarnation. Now that I have briefly defined karma we can explore "Karmonic Experience."

Karmonic Experience is a *predestined* life plan designed to process and fulfill a given life order. An individual's life experience is enhanced by free will by way of dynamic changes instituted by one's actions. This qualifies one to live in the initial life plan or, by way of action outside of one's natural path, can produce a new plan that in some cases changes the original Karmonic Experience. In other words, if one does not live within his/her natural process one can affect the outcome of what he/she was originally supposed to experience to enhance his/her awareness to God Consciousness.

Let us design a hypothetical action that is out of one's character to demonstrate the idea of how the process of Karmonic Experience works. For example, if I were to purposely rob a bank I would go to jail for ten years or more. As a result my personality would change due to my need to develop survival tactics for prison life. I would then come out a totally different person, perhaps ruthless and callous, upon the date of my release. My Karmonic Experience states that I would never have propagated an action such as robbing a bank, since it is not in my nature to do so. But by committing such an act purposely by way of free will, to prove this point, I would have changed my Karmonic Experience and now have a new life process experience. This action may detour me from my original spiritual evolution, which in turn has now, due to the unfavorable events, become my actual Karmonic Experience. We are to stay on course within our life plan with the help of our spirit guides, but through free will, it is possible to change.

In his book *Conversations with God*, Neale D. Walsh talks of mastering the game of life by starting over again like playing various levels of a video game to gain more experience. We can submit the idea that a video game — representing one's Karmonic Experience — can be played with different outcomes by the same player. These possible outcomes will be affected by the emotional state (free will) of the player during the game or perhaps by one's ability to gain specific skills every time we play (multiple reincarnations). To say the least different factors affect one's score every time one plays. It is the same video game, in this case representing the life process; however the same player can have many different outcomes when affected by free will. Yet, at the end of the game (life) the final outcome was to be as such, meaning one's true Karmonic Experience will play itself out.

Through free will we can change outcomes in our lives. However, the final outcome will be the ultimate one that was previously designed by us along with spirit guides. This was planned before we incarnated in order to learn specific teachings to reach a higher spiritual consciousness. By listening to one's spirit guide one can stay on course.

Divine Intervention is a manifestation of guidance, keeping us on our Karmonic path in order to gain as much as possible from our original life plan. If one understands the law of karma, one will find there is no other destiny than that of our natural will. The dichotomy is that free will keeps you on or off your life process within the Karmonic Experience. Confused yet? Let us investigate this further.

How do we qualify the effects of phenotype (environmental factors) and genotype (biological hereditary traits) influences when dictating our developmental process, which is supposed to be in tandem with our life plan? For example, monozygotic (i.e., identical) twins share identical genotypes since their genomes are the same, but they differ in phenotype. One can be shy while the other is outgoing. Although they are identical twins their life plans will be different.

Psychologists and social psychologists study positive and/or negative experiences within our home environment, using empirical research to qualify behavioral actions as normal or abnormal according to societal standards. They have found strong influences on behavior that can be reliably predicted from environmental effects on development. With that in mind, it is our will, or how we deal with the effects of our environment, negative or positive, that is processed and leads us to a joyful or disgruntled life.

To understand the grand scheme of life we need to understand the balance in life. That is, in order to have balance there must be supportive roles. For example, the heart, lungs, kidneys, and other organs are all individually designed to support the center, or common purpose, which is your life. All organs are functioning in their own right — having minds of their own — giving of themselves to be a creative part of the whole (you) for *all* of you to experience life. However, they (organs) are affected by what you eat, levels of stress, alcohol, tobacco, drugs, how you take care of your health. The organs will have to *learn* to live with what they are presented with in order to have balance (life).

With that in mind, we must learn to use our creativity to accept experiences of disharmony and negativity, whether they come in the form of other people or disasters. Not all of us are meant to be rich, beautiful to the eye, or famous. The more energy we spend on what will not be, or is not meant to be (not within our Karmonic Experience), the more miserable we will become. This does not mean we can't be creative and find our way out of poverty or do what it takes to improve our health or appearance. It means we are capable of reaching spiritual awareness by staying in control and listening to our spirit guides. By doing so we will live a joyful and fulfilling life.

Each of us, born into a specific situation, for reasons that are foreign to us, holds a vital key to what we are to learn in this lifetime. How we play out our experiences will affect our ability to manifest awareness to the purpose of our lives. Learning to accept our situation in a loving way is the pathway to reaching true joy. Therefore, *joy* is love. When you are at your hour of death, how rich, beautiful, popular, successful, or even how intelligent you are will mean little to you. What is important and will stand out is the people you love and how important that love is to you. There really aren't any secrets; but if you seek one then I will give it away: *Love is Life and Life is Love.*

The concept of love as part of the balance is necessary in order for a person who experiences negativity to be able to accept it, work his/her way out of it and evolve to a higher awareness — spirit consciousness. Moreover, not everyone is meant to gain spiritual awareness (or at least not all in the same lifetime). There are those who are to play a supporting role for others who are to reach a higher state of awareness. This is the balance that I am referring to, which is within the Divine plan.

Hitler and his followers are a good example of individuals whose negative actions fulfilled their role in history, thereby teaching us the importance and value of love and peace. I use this example to express how people have different Karmonic Experiences, with some Germans performing evil acts while others saved lives by aiding and hiding German Jews. The actions of some individuals, good or bad, shape the process of Karmonic Experience for others as well as themselves. Some people help to form the Karmonic Experience of others, who are to experience positive or negative events in order to evolve spiritually. If one is Buddhist then this also involves karma leading into a positive or negative rebirth depending on one's actions in a previous life.

To understand Divinity we must not limit our representation of what God is. Perhaps it would serve us to not limit the identifying representation of what "is" when we use the word "God." Many different theories explain *who* or *what* God is, and each enforces parameters to fulfill *its own* representation of what reality is in order to worship.

There is no difference when one worships idols made of clay, or when one worships an idea that God is singular and/or an identifiable character. We simply don't know other than through faith what God is. Therefore, I feel we must consider the idea of God as the ultimate representation of unconditional love and as having creative abilities either from this dimension, another dimension, or from another cosmos.

One should not be limited to the idea that God is a representation of what we need in order to be comforted and to fulfill our beliefs. For the purpose of this book the term "God" represents unconditional love and Divine Consciousness. Moreover, God will be identified as the common denominator of mankind and of the natural world in order to sustain all aspects of nature.

Many theologians would argue that nature is a grand design, and therefore there must be a designer. Could this designer possibly be an extraterrestrial life-form that some people refer to as aliens or ETs? Should we limit who or what this designer is by labeling its representation as an absolute? One could even argue *who* created the designer. We simply don't know — yet.

Divinity is a supportive process of creativity to everything that is in a state of being. When the Creator/Creators created humans, products of that creation were the mind, body, and spirit, which together have the ability to evoke and influence thought, and in turn produce the ability to create.

We are also creators but in a more simplistic form. By the use of thought we can create and manifest negative or positive experiences. But at times, we are not privy to the profundity that divinity plays in implanting a thought within us. Divine spirit guides offer personal guidance to enlightenment. This telepathic communication, which I refer to as Induced Knowledge, gives information in the form of a thought attached to the knowledge or feeling that something is "as such" or "will happen," and then the very thought does "come true." Some call it premonition or a gut feeling when one thinks about a friend and a few seconds later the phone rings, and it is that very person he/she was thinking of. The person thinking about his or her friend will state it was a coincidence and will not attempt to investigate this type of phenomenon any further. *Déjà vu* is a feeling that one has previously felt or experienced something before. In the case of this phenomenon, we use language to satisfy our curiosity; reducing the experience to what we know as "déjà vu" ends any further investigation of the phenomenon.

The term "divinity" is in itself loosely defined. It has varied meanings to different people and within different beliefs. To some, it can mean "transcendental power"; it can be another word for the "Holy Spirit"; or it can mean Divine Will or Divine Retribution bringing justice to evildoers. Mormons define "divinity" as the extent of human capacity or potential, as is the divine potential of mankind. Some will say divinity is a representation of a singular entity as practiced by a monotheistic faith (one God), while others apply it to mean God Consciousness.

Regardless of how divinity is interpreted, it is a representation of anything that is Godlike. Therefore, during an experience of Divine Intervention, one is in the act of communion with the Divine Source. It is a spiritual connection with purity and love. It is an expression of the true self, which is why I stress the awareness of communication from the Divinity. It will serve the purpose of enhancing the individual's Karmonic Experience. Learn to recognize it and embrace it for all its glory in aiding you to reach a higher level of spirit consciousness.

I am fortunate to have had experiences of Divine Intervention, which have proven to me how an actual spiritual encounter can affect one's life. In my case it presented miracles in my life, which allowed me to survive potential danger. With each experience of Divine Intervention I learned to recognize and appreciate this type of communion with the Creator or spirit guides. I have found it a loving relationship, and I am here to share its value with you.

Don Pablo Alvarez
The Wise Helper Along the Path

"For me there is only the traveling on the paths that have a heart, on any path that may have a heart. There I travel, and the only worthwhile challenge for me is to traverse its full length. And there I travel — looking, looking, breathlessly."

CARLOS CASTANEDA, *THE TEACHINGS OF DON JUAN*

On July 18, 1992, my sister, brother, and sister in-law flew from Los Angeles to El Paso, Texas — our final destination was Artesia, New Mexico. We were on our way to bury my grandfather Calletano Heredia Alvarado, born in Redford, Texas, on August 10, 1895; he passed on July 16, 1992. C. H., the name my grandfather was known by, lived in Marfa, Texas, before moving to Artesia, New Mexico, where he finally settled and lived to the age of ninety-seven. He was an old-time cowboy at heart and a very special person in my life. But most of all he represented a romantic era, that dying breed of the authentic cowboy. He and his three brothers, Juan, Pablo, and Jose Alvarado, were born in the late 1800s. They lived to be old men, each with his own cowboy tales of adventure.

The Alvarado brothers were young cowboys working cattle for ranchers and farmers in Texas and New Mexico to support themselves and their families. My people are a mixture of Mexicans, Spaniards, and Comanche Native Americans who lived and roamed the area of the Pecos River. The homeland of these inhabitants ranged from Presidio and Marfa, Texas, up to Carlsbad, Artesia, and Roswell, New Mexico.

This area is rich with Southwestern history including the Lincoln County Wars, the infamous outlaw Billy the Kid, and Comanche raids. The Comanche named the

Mescalero Apache Puberty Feast, Kimberly Enjady (middle) (by Richard Alaniz).

Pecos River "the foul tasting river," and it formed the natural boundary separating the Mescalero Apache to the west from the Kwahadi (Antelope-Eaters) Comanche (*Numunu*) to the east. The Spaniards who were the first invaders of New Mexico and Texas were no match for the fierce Comanche warriors, who were experts on horseback and became the feared "Lords of the Southern Plains" controlling all of Texas and part of eastern New Mexico. According to historians, it was common knowledge that if you mentioned the name "Comanche" to white settlers it would cause them to "shiver in their boots." Many of these settlers died at the end of a spear or swift arrow of a Comanche protecting his homeland. Because the Comanche were expert horsemen they could cover large areas of land to secure it for a tribe that was made up of thirty-five different bands. They were known for breeding and developing prize horse herds that were often traded to other tribes as a commercial enterprise.

After the Spaniards were defeated, the Comanche interbred with captive Mexicans and Spaniards, and with time, there was a new race of people living along the Pecos River. This new mixed race of people — for survival reasons — eventually chose to embrace the Mexican way of life, speaking only Spanish, to distinguish themselves from the Comanches. At that time white bounty hunters were paid for Native

Mescalero Apache Crown Dancers (by Erica Alaniz).

American scalps: $100 for males, $50 for females, and $25 for a child. Regardless if one was an Apache, Comanche, or Yaqui, if you had long dark hair you were killed for your scalp. The struggle of this land is the history of my people — the Pecos River People.

My cousin Art "Tudy" Garcia met us at the airport in El Paso. He volunteered to drive us to Artesia for the funeral of my grandfather C. H. While en route our conversation turned to the topic of spirituality, and at that very moment we were passing the majestic Guadalupe Peak. The Guadalupe Mountain range runs north and south from New Mexico and partially into Texas where Guadalupe Peak is located. As we passed this beautiful mountain range that also happened to be our ancestral hunting grounds, I directed our discussion to the story of the Mescalero Apache mountain spirits. As told to me by a Mescalero Apache medicine man, the mountain spirits were given to the Apaches in a cave located at a high point on Guadalupe Peak.

A large part of Mescalero Apache spirituality centers around the Puberty Feast, held annually on July 4th. After the "Indian Wars," many Native Americans were incarcerated on reservations by the U.S. Government, and any form of religious ceremony was outlawed. After much protest, the government allowed the Apaches to practice their maiden ceremony but only on the 4th of July in an attempt to "Americanize" what was depicted by Christian ideology as a "heathen" ceremony.

Today, in addition to the annual July 4th feast, private feasts are allowed anytime during the year in the back country of the reservation where large groups of tribal Apache members celebrate their traditional ways.

The annual July 4th Puberty Feast is open to the public before eleven o'clock in the evening, and non-Indians are asked to leave after that time. The private feast is open to all tribal members but is closed to outsiders unless one is invited to attend by an Apache.

The Puberty Feast is an eight-day celebration and includes many traditional ceremonies. The first four days everyone is offered a meal consisting of traditional foods whereas the last four days are only for the maidens and their immediate families.

According to legend, the Mescalero Crown Dancers (mountain spirits) were given to an Apache medicine woman. She had a vision that directed her to go to a cave located at Guadalupe Peak, Texas. After her vision and experience in the cave she returned to her tribe to report her vision and what she had learned from the spirits that appeared to her. While in the cave she was told to teach the men how to dress and dance according to the spirits' instructions. This ritual dance is still performed to this day in tandem with the coming-of-age maiden ceremony within the *Big Tipi*.

The feast ground where tribal members come for blessings and participate in traditional customs is blessed and considered sacred. The main ceremony is held in the sacred Medicine Tipi or *Big Tipi* as it is sometimes referred to. It is constructed of brush and large lodge poles where the young Apache girls dance for their puberty ritual.

The Crown Dancers perform their dance around a large bonfire to the rhythm of singers and drummers. This is separate from what is transpiring in the *Big Tipi*. I spent many years as an apprentice standing behind medicine people learning the chants and protocol within the *Big Tipi* as they used rattles and sang sacred songs.

Tudy was impressed with my knowledge of Apache spirituality, which I acquired during my visits to Mescalero. He then spoke of Don Pablo Alvarez, a knowledgeable *curandero* (spiritual healer) living in Artesia. Don Pablo, as many in Artesia referred to him, was in his late eighties and ill with cancer. Tudy was not sure if Don Pablo was still alive, but mentioned that our cousin Robert "Bobby" Villa would know more about Don Pablo, his condition, and how to locate him.

At that moment I had an intuitive feeling Don Pablo might help me in making sense of my encounters with the paranormal. Perhaps he would be able to shed light on the experience I had when my father appeared to me after his passing. All I knew was I had a strong desire and compulsion to meet Don Pablo. I felt my connection with him would play an important part in my life. In retrospect, it was the beginning of acknowledging a profound spiritual journey.

At 3:00 p.m. on Sunday, July 19, 1992, our family gathered at the mortuary for my grandfather's viewing. After everyone had cleared the room, I stood in front of his open casket, burned some sage and blessed my two sisters, sister-in-law, myself, my grandfather's body, and finally the six directions pertaining to the casket with *Tah-dah-din* (yellow cattail pollen, used by Apaches for blessing). After the blessing I placed a beautiful bone choker that I made for my grandfather upon his neck.

I then unfolded a sharp Buck knife out of my pocket and asked my sister to cut my hair off just below the rubber band that secured my long ponytail. I tied the long strands that were once a part of me in leather and included an eagle feather and a medicine bundle as I said a prayer for my grandfather's journey to the spirit world. I then placed it under his coat next to his heart so I could retrieve it when I joined him and my other ancestors in the spirit world.

After we laid my grandfather to rest I saw Bobby Villa in a crowd of people and decided to approach him and inquire about Don Pablo Alvarez. I asked him if Don Pablo was still alive and if it was possible to meet with him. Although Bobby knew Don Pablo was in ill health he knew he was still alive and would probably be able to see us.

As we turned off the highway and drove down the unpaved driveway of Don Pablo's home I was reminded of a passage in Carlos Castaneda's book, *The Teachings of Don Juan,* where he describes his first encounter with his spiritual guide, Don Juan. Like Mr. Castaneda, I didn't know what to expect from my visit, but I knew there was a purpose.

With every footstep leading up to Don Pablo's door, anticipation increased, and I wondered what this spiritual healer/*curandero* looked like and how he would comport himself. When my foot eased upon the doorstep I discarded any expectation or preconceived notion I had of him. Only seconds stood between me and Don Pablo — I needed to be mentally prepared.

Tristine Chico's Puberty Feast, Stephanie Chico (l.), the author (r.) (by Truett Chico).

Bobby and I were greeted by his daughter Guadalupe, and as I entered their home my eyes were directed to Don Pablo's physical presence. The mental images of the last few hours were transformed.

There sat an aging thin man with a large frame sitting in a recliner placed next to a large picture window with an unobstructed view of the outside world. I noticed he was blind in his right eye and his vision in the left eye seemed to be failing him even though he wore glasses. The thick-lensed glasses resting on the bridge of his nose were the only visual connection Don Pablo had to his visitor who was approaching him reverently, as a student approaches his master.

He welcomed me after Bobby introduced us and acknowledged he knew my family. He invited me to sit next to him. You have probably seen an elderly person at a rest home sitting with an empty gaze and an aging body only waiting for the wind of time to carry his or her soul away. However, as Don Pablo spoke, his mind was active and animated. He seemed as curious to meet me as I was to meet him.

He used his large hands in a slow manner as he talked. He spoke in what we call "Spanglish," a mixture of English and Spanish that is the common way of communication in the Pecos River region. We talked of his spiritual training, his knowledge of herbs, the use of crystal balls, and the power he received to heal the sick by laying of hands in the name of Jesus.

I asked Don Pablo if it was possible for a spirit to come in solid form, as we are when we are alive. He responded with a story about a close friend of his, Alberto Muniz, nicknamed "Salude." This nickname was given to Alberto because when he would see Don Pablo he would always say aloud and drag out the word, "Saaaaluuude!" Don Pablo stated he was preparing to visit some people outside of Artesia, and he was going to be out of town for about a week. He was going up to the second story of a building where he was visiting when to his surprise his friend Salude approached him. They greeted one another, and Salude made him laugh as always. After a brief conversation his dear friend Salude said his good-byes and departed.

Later when Don Pablo returned to Artesia, his son, a police officer in Artesia, called his father on the phone to give him the sad news. His dear friend Salude was killed in an auto accident earlier that week. Don Pablo argued it was impossible and his son must have been mistaken because he had seen and spoken to Salude just the other day. The truth was Salude had been killed earlier that week. Don Pablo then realized it was Salude's spirit who had visited with him to say his last farewell. He described him to be in human form, solid, and very much alive — he even shook his hand. He has witnessed people come from the dead before, so this was not an unusual experience for Don Pablo. He shared another story of this type of experience when a spirit sometimes will return to comfort a loved one.

He recounted a story of a woman who, like many others before her, had come to Don Pablo for assistance. She reported that her daughter, Beatrice, was very sick, and she pleaded for him to help her. Many people had come to Don Pablo for spiritual healing and laying of the hands. Don Pablo referred to himself as an instrument of God and explained that his healing powers were from God. At Beatrice's mother's request he went to her house to see what he could do for the bedridden daughter.

Don Pablo found the daughter had been dead for at least fourteen hours with the body showing signs of rigor mortis. He tried to explain that her daughter was deceased. With the continuing pleas of the mother for him to save her daughter, Don Pablo asked her for a cup of water and a spoon. He used the spoon to help pry open the daughter's mouth so he could pour a spoonful of water inside. She did not gag. He was trying to convince the mother her daughter was truly dead and it was impossible for the daughter not to gag with water in her mouth if she was alive.

The mother cried hysterically and refused to believe her daughter was dead. She pleaded with Don Pablo to pray for her daughter and to cure her with a healing. As Don Pablo was praying, Beatrice miraculously placed her hand on top of Don Pablo's. She opened her eyes to look at him. The mother told Don Pablo in Spanish that she knew all along her daughter had not died and was full of joy as she praised God. The girl spoke and said she had died but came back to tell her mother she was okay. She explained to her mother that as soon as she released Don Pablo's hand she would return to where she had just come from. She asked her mother not to worry and told her that she loved her. As soon as Beatrice let go of Don Pablo's hand, she died once again.

Don Pablo explained there are many ways in which spirits communicate with us, and the experience with my father was not only real but had a profound purpose. Don Pablo talked about having the ability to put his hand through a solid wall, saying this was possible because certain areas in our dimension are known as doors or openings. These areas are known to many as portals to the spiritual world or other dimensions.

Then Don Pablo said he had a message for me. I was to leave the Apache way of spirituality alone, meaning I should advance beyond them. I was shocked he knew I was training in the medicine ways on the Apache reservation as well as with other indigenous cultures. According to Don Pablo, I had a higher calling directly with the celestial Godhead. Perhaps he may have not meant God himself but, rather, the celestial realm. He said I would limit my growth if I were to continue to practice solely in the manner I was adhering to. He continued, "You will advance to a different knowledge, to a higher spirituality, you are being guided by a highly evolved spirit guide," emphasizing it was important for me to move forward.

Through Don Pablo's message, I learned that intention should be supported with trust in one's experiences and to accept the existence of multidimensional beings that are to guide us to spirit consciousness. It was not until later I understood the value of the guidance and message Don Pablo had given me. Soon after my visit with Don Pablo, I decided to focus on a higher spiritual awareness with the guidance from my spirit guide as Don Pablo instructed. There was nothing wrong with being a shaman, but I was convinced Apaches should be the only people allowed in the *Big Tipi* as medicine men. Non-Apaches should be excluded, to keep their tradition pure and free from outside intervention.

I wanted another visit with Don Pablo to record his personal experiences and to document his life story. Luckily Bobby offered to drive me to the airport the following day. Don Pablo granted my request and was willing to let us interview him, understanding a record of his life story was important. I planned to take a video recorder with me to document my final visit with him so I could capture visual images that could accompany my notes.

Biography

On my second visit with Don Pablo I was allowed to videotape him, and with my notes from the previous day's visit I compiled this biography, dated July 21, 1992:

Don Pablo was born Pablo Alvarez in 1904 in the city of Pecos, Texas, located in Rivers County. When he was three or four, his family relocated to Artesia, New Mexico. At the age of twenty-nine he wandered out into the surrounding desert and declared himself a servant of God after he had a spiritual revelation.

An angel appeared to him while he was in the desert and told him he would have a gift of healing from God. Although Don Pablo was perplexed by his encounter with the angel, he knew his life would change in a profound way. It was revealed to him his life would include much suffering. The angel told him he would spend one year in prison, would be denounced by the Catholic Church for practicing his healing powers, and two of his sons would die at the will of his enemies. All of this came to pass in the coming years.

In 1930 he received a certificate from the Sage Institute in Paris, France. I actually saw this document myself when I was interviewing him. It was in that year Don Pablo began his healing practice by primarily laying of his hands and secondarily using herbs for medicinal and spiritual healings. He also mentioned the use of a crystal ball on occasion. Don Pablo was excommunicated from the Catholic Church for practicing what the church called "witchcraft." He was accused by the church of being a *brujo* (a sorcerer who practices witchcraft).

Don Pablo's first wife, Teresa Alvarez, gave birth to their only daughter, Guadalupe, and their first son, Pedro, who died at the age of eleven months. Teresa died when their second son, Pablo Jr., was two years old. His second wife, Carolina, helped raise Pablo Jr. until he died at the age of six, fulfilling the prophecy that Don Pablo would lose two sons. He and Carolina had three more sons together, Cruz, Alfredo, and Eduardo. Cruz received his Ph.D, and he learned the healing aspects of herbs from his father before Don Pablo passed to the spirit world.

In 1976 Don Pablo took ill, and in 1978 he chose to go to the Holy Land in Jerusalem to bathe in the Jordan River. While in the Jordan River Don Pablo prayed and asked God for a miracle. He asked for God to turn the water from cold to hot. He mentioned that the other tourists were amazed that as soon as Don Pablo walked out of the river, his shorts were dry, and everyone else's swimsuits were wet. According to Don Pablo this was the miracle that God gave him. He visited the tombs of Jesus and Lazarus in Jericho and also walked the path that Jesus walked when he carried his cross. In 1983 Don Pablo traveled to the Vatican where he visited and talked with Pope John Paul II.

Some people where he lived did not understand him or his abilities. His enemies chose to label Don Pablo a *brujo*. But people who came from all over for a healing knew him as a healer praising the name of Jesus for his powers to heal the sick.

Before he passed he mentioned to my cousin Bobby that he knew some men were coming for him and he would be leaving in the very near future, meaning his passing was soon. He was happy we collected information on his life. Don Pablo Alvarez transitioned to the spirit world on March 18, 1993. I was fortunate to not only experience his presence, but to document his life as a spiritual healer.

Teachings of Don Pablo

After I left Don Pablo and flew home on July 22, 1992, four events happened to me that I know were a result of my encounter with him.

The first occurred when we were landing in Phoenix, Arizona, for a layover and plane change. We almost crashed as the plane hit the ground with a very hard landing that really shook everyone up. I had flown in just about every military aircraft, yet landing in Phoenix was the worst experience I had ever had. I looked over to my sister-in-law and told her I was thinking of Don Pablo as we were making the extremely rough landing. My sister-in-law asked me not to think about any of that "stuff," as she called it; she was concerned because we still had another plane to catch to Los Angeles. We experienced a calm and uneventful flight to Los Angeles Airport.

The second unusual experience I had was when I arrived back at my studio from the airport in Los Angeles. When I entered my building I attempted to turn on the lights with no success. I checked the fuse box inside the building and the main power box outside, and then checked with my neighbors to see if the entire block was blacked out. I found it was only my building that was without power. My next move was to call the electric company to report the problem.

The operator had me go through a mandatory seven-step process before she would send out a crew. I informed her I had already completed the process several times before I called but she insisted we go through it again. It failed, and I was still without electricity. The operator scheduled a crew to come out to my place. An hour passed, and the crew finally showed up. The first procedure they attempted was to turn off and on the breaker switch in the main box located outside the building. The lights came on and I felt like a fool as I explained to them I had done that about six different times without any success. They said perhaps there was a short and I should replace the switch. I should mention at the time of this writing I have not ever replaced that breaker switch and it has been over fifteen years since this incident occurred, and I have never had any problems since.

The following morning, July 23, I was getting ready to open my studio when a third event happened. I was picturing in my mind a customer of mine by the name of Gilbert standing at my doorway wearing a solid red long-sleeved shirt with blue jeans. There was a maroon-colored pickup truck that I could see parked outside at the curb but only the front bumper and part of the hood was visible to me. I was curious as to why I would be thinking about this person because Gilbert would only do business with me once or twice a year compared to my regular clients who came on monthly visits. I brushed the mental image off and didn't think of it any further until a few minutes later when I heard someone call out my name.

Gilbert was standing at my doorway wearing a red long-sleeved shirt with jeans. Behind him I could see the front end of a maroon truck exactly how I pictured them both in my mind just a few minutes earlier. I was totally amazed by what I was experiencing and mentioned to Gilbert I was just thinking about him. In reality, I was not only thinking about him, I was picturing him in my mind exactly as he was postured at the door entrance.

I have experienced déjà vu before, but this was something different. I was picturing an event mentally and seeing it occur before it actually happened. I went into the future for a few moments — a psychic vision is what I was actually experiencing — what Richard H. Robinson, author of *The Buddhist Religion*, refers to as the "fifth superknowledge," "the divine eye" or "psychic vision."

The concept of time is manmade, according to Albert Einstein. His Theory of Relativity states all experiences are happening at the same moment, and time is relative to one's experience. I was guided to tune in to a relative time phenomenon for a reason I did not understand.

The fourth event needs special attention because it is the most profound and unifies all of the experiences. As my client Gilbert and I were conducting business, a wild dove flew through my studio entrance. This occurred about ten minutes after I had my vision of Gilbert standing at the front door. Gilbert commented he did not realize I kept birds in my building, surprised that the bird flew in and landed on a stuffed hawk that was mounted on the wall with its wings spread open. The wild dove, which is high on the hawk's food chain, happened to land right on the shoulder of the hawk's wing. I could not fathom what was actually happening. I was trying to tie everything together but there was more to come that was even more mystifying and strange.

I went over to my prayer shrine, lit some sage, and said a brief prayer to acknowledge the event. I asked what the dove's entrance represented. I knew it was not just coincidence. I had been in that building for over twenty years and never had any animal, let alone a bird, walk or fly into my place of business.

I immediately closed the front door and finished my business with Gilbert, who was anxious to leave; he was concerned after I went to my prayer shrine. I observed the wild dove fly over to the direction of the door that he had entered and land on the air-conditioning unit positioned above the door. It then flew back to the hawk and landed on the exact same spot on the wing as to reinstate its purpose, or perhaps to get me to acknowledge further this was a message of some sort.

The prayer shrine is very simple with pictures of my relatives who have passed and an abalone shell in which I place the residue of burnt incense or sage. Next to and above my pictures I have on the wall a three-foot woven group of sticks bound by the leaves of a Spanish dagger yucca plant used as twine. This weaving together is called a "Thousand and One Lights" by the Mescalero Apaches. The stick was used by medicine men to light their cigarettes from the fire pit that was deep in the ground in the middle of the *Big Tipi*. Apaches use cigarettes made of herbs as a personal blessing as other tribes would use a sacred red stone pipe.

Any article used in the *Big Tipi* during a ceremony is considered sacred — it was presented to me. I hung it next to the shrine to remind me of the Mescalero Apaches and their medicine ways. Every morning I light sage or incense and remember my family members who have passed, and pray for wellness and good health for those who are living. It is my way to acknowledge my friends and family who have transitioned to the spirit world and to keep them in my life.

I looked up at the dove, and without warning, it flew over to the shrine and landed on the top of the "Thousand and One Lights," sliding down, wings flapping for balance as its claws glided down to the bottom of the stick, ending up in the shell. The dove faced me, perched in the abalone shell that was located directly under the stick. Amazed by this event, I felt it must be some type of message.

Was the spirit world using this wild bird to communicate with me? Was it Don Pablo making a magical connection to elicit a response from me? Or could it be what one would call a mere coincidence?

I approached the dove, directed my attention toward the bird, and said, "Were you sent by Don Pablo? If so, then what is your reason or your message?" Of course no form of telepathy from the bird or physical response was given. I felt ridiculous trying to talk to a bird, so I decided to take a break from this strange experience by making a trip to the bank. I would deal with all of this later.

When I returned from the bank I proceeded to look for the dove. I almost tore my studio apart, but the bird was nowhere to be found. I became frustrated because I was not fond of having tricks played on me. I began to think the bird disappeared into thin air. But how was that possible? What other explanation was there? I was able to accept anything after what I had experienced over the last couple of days. So much was happening in a short time span, and all of it had transpired after my visit with Don Pablo.

My search for the dove proved fruitless, so I decided to quench my thirst at the water cooler. As I was walking toward the cooler I was thinking about going to my desk immediately afterward to balance my checkbook. Just as I turned around from the water cooler the dove flew in front of me, circled around my studio, and landed on the chair at my desk where just moments before I was thinking of sitting. I became frustrated. I thought, "That's it for me! Game over! No more of this spiritual stuff." I wanted a normal life with normal events. This was too much in such a short period — I wanted immediate answers.

I approached and grabbed the dove, but once in my hands it fought to free itself. I took it outside, blessed it, and released it. It landed on a telephone wire facing me, then flew directly southeast toward Artesia, New Mexico, from where I had just come.

All of these events happened on Wednesday, and on the following Saturday of the same week I decided to visit a friend in Corona for the weekend. When I exited the back door of my studio I noticed a large pile of bird droppings on the back porch step. It seemed odd because I had never seen bird droppings on that particular concrete step in all the years I had occupied the building. I looked to see if a bird was perched on top of the roof and for signs of a trail of the droppings on the wall next to the steps. There was nothing, so I didn't think anything more of it and left for the weekend.

I returned to my studio the following Monday. When I approached the back door there was a dead dove in the exact spot where the bird droppings were before I left. I could tell the dove had recently died because rigor mortis had not set in. If the bird had been there for a long duration the ants would have already been feasting. I decided to bless the bird and bury it so it could return to the Earth. But most of all to show respect for the possible role it played in giving me a profound experience with the spirit world.

I called Bobby Villa, in Artesia, and told him what had transpired. I asked him to retell my story to Don Pablo and to find what meaning it represented. A few days later, Bobby reported that Don Pablo explained the dove was a messenger from the spirit world. It was a sign telling me to leave the Apache way of spiritual practice alone, supporting what he was told to tell me during my visit with him. There was a higher calling for me, and I was not to be sidetracked with any other concepts of spirituality. I was to have many experiences that would guide me for a purpose that would be revealed to me later. He also stated the spirit world uses animals, people, and events such as this to help guide us. I was to evolve to a higher state of spirituality and my life was to change *forever*.

Because of my experience and guidance from Don Pablo, I was placed in a deferent state of freedom and awareness. It conditioned me to look beyond the acceptable realities that have been given to us in order to find truth. In time, I found the truth is within our reach. We simply have to free ourselves, open our senses, and take a quantum leap. I dedicate this chapter to the incredible life of Don Pablo Alvarez and to his work, which gave me my personal spiritual freedom.

S E V E N

Spiritual Webbing
Instantaneous Interconnectivity with Others

"It is possible that the next Buddha will not take the form of an individual.
The next Buddha may take the form of a community — a community practicing
understanding and loving kindness, a community practicing mindful living. This
may be the most important thing we can do for the survival of the earth."

THICH NHAT HANH

Spiritual Webbing is a process by which two or more people cross paths to gain
an experience of spiritual purpose either of a small significance or of a profound
life-changing nature. There will be many individuals who will come into your life
offering guidance for your spiritual maturity. Sometimes it will be subtle and other
times it will be grand enough to awaken your conscious mind to shift your personal
philosophy. Your current ideology may be altered by the experience of Spiritual
Webbing. Carl Jung (1875–1961), founder of analytical psychology, would categorize such experiences as *synchronicity*.

I have found that God and/or the spirit world have brought people into my
life, even if for a brief moment, to be influenced by words that have planted a seed.
This seed begins their process of spiritual growth. I look back and can truly say
the same has happened for me upon crossing paths with others who have brought
with them a message to point me in the right direction, thereby influencing my
spiritual consciousness.

The spirit world connects with us in many forms, including words either from
a conversation, song lyrics, poem, or any type of communication used to influence us. I have personally experienced this phenomenon, where the paths of two

individuals cross so that one or both will experience Divine Intervention through Spiritual Webbing. This type of experience supports my theory that webbing connects us with certain people so we may serve each other in a profound way.

I was among a group of Native American actors who were hired to work for a French pizza commercial in Sedona, Arizona. Famous for its majestic red rock formations, Sedona has become the preferred site of many film productions due to its scenic landscape.

After "wrapping" the three-day production shoot, we prepared to return to our hotel. It was announced that a van was leaving at 11:00 p.m. to visit one of the six Vortex power spots located in Sedona as a bonus sightseeing tour since we finished filming ahead of schedule. One of the crewmembers, who was of Iranian decent, approached me and asked if I planned on going. I was undecided due to my fatigue and told him if I decided to go, I would meet everyone at the van.

A few minutes after 11:00 p.m. the young Iranian fellow knocked at my hotel door and was almost insisting that I go. I assured him I would meet everyone at the van but I was curious why he was so adamant. As I approached the meeting spot, only one woman, who was the production driver, and the Iranian gentleman were waiting at the van. Upon seeing there were only two people, I figured they would cancel the outing, but he insisted that we still go.

On the way to the Vortex our conversation turned to the subject of spirituality and a specific experience the young man was having. He said he had a gut feeling he would find an explanation there at the Vortex for his recurring dream. I asked him to give a basic description of the dream. He shared that on many occasions he would wake up drenched in sweat because he saw a *demon* attacking him. Every time he tried to leave the room to get away from the demon he would be attacked by a half-man, half-animal creature that would block his exit. Even though the demon didn't hurt him in any way, he would not allow him to leave his room by either blocking his exit or holding him back.

Since dreams can be symbolic I asked if he had experienced anything in his waking life that might have some relation to the dream. He responded by saying his family was wealthy, and they wanted him to be involved in the family business. However, much to the dismay of his parents, he had chosen a life in the film industry. I felt there must be something deeper; therefore, I asked him if he was involved with anything else that may be *unusual* or novel. With widened eyes, he admitted, "I'm involved with a film crew who will go to Mexico to film a Yaqui peyote ceremony in the near future, and I am very excited to be part of it."

I told him involvement in any ceremony that requires ingesting peyote could be potentially dangerous for a novice who has no idea of its purpose. I felt there could be negative physical and emotional consequences for him if he were to participate.

Peyote is a cactus that contains a hallucinogen. The Yaqui Indians of Northern Mexico make a tea by boiling the cactus buttons. This tea is then consumed in order to reach a higher level of consciousness and to relate to the spirit world. There is an indigenous saying: "The white man goes to church to pray to God; the Indian eats peyote and talks to God." The deity that is manifested from drinking the potion is of territorial spirituality; a locally practiced belief system indigenous people have passed on from many generations before.

When under the influence of such a powerful hallucinogen my new friend could have experienced irreversible damage to his mental well-being, especially if he was not emotionally stable. Although there are many people who have experienced eating or drinking peyote without any harm, I felt his experience would probably not go well. I understood at this moment his spirit guides placed me in his life to help him veer off this course of potential self-destruction and protect his mental senses or perhaps his physical health.

A few minutes later we reached our destination, and the three of us disembarked the van, and in the darkness proceeded to hike up a large hill where the Vortex was located. Once we reached the general area of the Vortex, the production driver went into a New Age practice of chanting. When she saw we were not joining in and perhaps not interested in what she was doing, she relocated to a secluded area so she could get connected on her own, in her own way.

My Iranian friend and I continued our conversation, and I had a feeling something of a profound nature was about to come of our experience together. I decided to bless him and myself before we continued any further. I hunted wild sage, harvested it ceremoniously, smoked us both, and recited a simple prayer to summon our spirit guides before asking him to describe his dream in detail.

His description of the demon was odd and at the same time interesting because of its half-man, half-animal nature. According to his description the demon had the head of an animal with three horns protruding from its crown, the face of a man, legs of an animal, and the chest of a human skeleton with its ribs exposed.

I asked him if the demon had hooves with four legs; he said the demon had two legs with no hooves but there were many thin worms dangling from the sides of its legs. I continued my questioning about the face of the demon hoping for a detailed account. He could not see the demon's face clearly because it was painted; but he knew it was the face of a man. As he said these last words, a clear mental picture of the demon came to me. I asked him if the right side was painted red, the left side black, and if there was a thin white line going down the middle from the forehead to the chin. He was surprised to hear my detailed narrative and immediately asked me, "How did you know?"

"Because I am the 'demon' in your dreams," I responded confidently. I explained I was not a demon at all, but sent by his spirit guide to discourage him from filming the peyote ceremony in Mexico. Seeing the look of puzzlement on his face, I continued to tell him his description of the demon was a portrayal of the way I am dressed and painted when I dance traditionally. I paint one side of my face red and the other side black with a white thin stripe down the middle. My medicine war shield I dance with is also painted with the same colors.

I wear a wolf's hide over my head with three eagle feathers pointing upward. My bare chest is covered with a bone breastplate, and my legs are covered with buckskin leggings. The leather fringe on the leggings is in the Comanche style, moistened then twisted, which gave it the appearance, at least to him, of worms protruding from the sides of my legs. This indigenous custom was foreign to him. He knew nothing about the way Native Americans dress in traditional fashion when dancing. Mine is of a traditional shield-and-lance war dancer.

I continued my explanation of his dream by describing how Spiritual Webbing works, and this type of webbing was not new for me. I realized we both had come full circle: he experienced me in his dreams so I could help direct him away from something his spirit guides wanted him to avoid.

He had a *gut* feeling, that of all the other participants who were involved with the film production, it was imperative to have me accompany him to the Vortex. He did not know what role I was to play, but he *knew* intuitively this place, and my connection to it, would provide him with the long-awaited explanation he had been seeking.

This young man experienced Induced Knowledge, Divine Intervention, and Spiritual Webbing in order to evolve and/or to be aware of the essence of spirituality.

I taught him how to bless himself and told him that in the medicine way he was to give me something of value for the role I played in helping him come full circle and find a path to healing and spirituality.

The following day we said our good-byes, and I could see a big change in him. He thanked me and presented me with a denim shirt — his favorite article of clothing. He stated he wished he could give me something more valuable but this was the best he could do with what little he had. I accepted the gift and knew the shirt was appropriate; but more importantly the gift symbolized his acceptance of the new knowledge that was given to him.

I advised him to never forget the profound experience the spirit world gave him, and it was his choice now to open his ears and heart to the wisdom of his spirit guides. By the look on his face I could tell he was amazed by all that had transpired as well as the weight that was lifted once he found answers to what had been bothering him for a long time.

The day I met Jennifer, my best friend and soul mate, I received a message from my silent voice that she would be a part of my life in a special way. I knew this was not going to be an ordinary "boy meets girl" encounter. Within forty-five minutes of our first meeting I knew this relationship was going to be extraordinary. Needless to say, I didn't tell her about my Induced Knowledge because I did not know if she was a spiritually conscious person. It was something I was going to keep a watch on to see how it would develop without pushing for a relationship.

Once Jennifer got to know me, and we developed a sense of trust, she shared with me she was deeply troubled with a dark side. In learning this I felt my purpose in her life was to help her heal herself. In turn I was to gain an even more profound experience through our Spiritual Webbing as well as a very loving relationship.

The details are very personal but I can tell you I was guided by my silent voice — my spirit guide. I was guided to help her find a way out from under her issues, while at the same time confirming for myself the existence and reality of a profound spiritual knowledge. Our relationship involves the purity of God's unconditional love, which inspired us to find joy in each other and is the root of our love and our marriage.

The experience of webbing transpires often in the work I do. My work has changed tremendously in guiding individuals to wellness of mind, body, and spirit. By way of teaching meditation and sharing my experiences, I, with the direction of my spirit guide, have been able to help others in their personal quest to alleviate depression, stress, anxiety attacks, low self-esteem, hopelessness, bereavement, and spiritual challenges that may be occurring in their lives.

My income has dropped tremendously since I have directed my life to helping others, but as a benefit, so has my ego. I am now in control of my life, and every time I need money to sustain myself it is presented to me in the most unexpected ways.

I know now "I" am responsible for my actions that affect my life. It is not God's will that I do well or not. However, I know I am not alone. My spirit guide, as well as others who come to me through Spiritual Webbing, are here to help me through my journey. I give value to my experiences and people who are dear to me in shaping my life.

How I have chosen to live is confusing to most people who know me. I am no longer interested in gaining large amounts of money or work toward gaining more *stuff* to make me happy. My reward in life is with each person in whom I have been able to bring forth an uplifting state of awareness and peace of mind. It truly is my bliss.

Listen well and study the interactions you have with people who may have an effect on your personal spirituality and the philosophy by which you live your life. You will find with time your encounter with these people ignited a flame, either small or large, to enhance your spiritual awareness.

Be open to accepting every good or bad experience so as to understand a lesson within each. If you can see the connection that ties them all together you will find your purpose in life as well as what you were to learn in this incarnation. We have all had an experience of Spiritual Webbing; it is up to you to recognize it and its teaching.

EIGHT

Spirit Riders of the Wind
Ancestral Spirit Helpers

"The first act of awe, when man was struck with the beauty or
wonder of Nature, was the first spiritual experience."
HENRYK SKOLIMOWSKI

This chapter is dedicated to my family members who love the horse and stay in
constant harmony with this majestic animal even after their passing. They are now
Spirit Riders, and the wind carries their hearts buoyed by the gentle rhythm that
only the horse can create; they are both harmoniously balanced only when each is
with the other.

A true horseman may feel heaven doesn't exist unless the horse also exists there
for the ultimate ride to carry one's spirit on the magnificent trail to the spirit world.
This is possible only if the cowboy is worthy and the horse is mighty to complete
the journey through the dimensions of time and space.

The horseback experience I developed as a youth and while riding with Apaches
in New Mexico fulfilled my innate passion for horses. Owning a few horses in Los
Angeles finally paid off in the form of a salary when I started working as a stuntman
for film and television.

While on location for one particular commercial, I experienced yet another
profound connection with the spirit world that was another gift of knowledge by
way of experience. This was the second visitation from someone related to me who
had passed away and then appeared to me in physical form.

The producers of the Discovery Channel were auditioning Native Americans with horse skills to ride bareback for a commercial that was to be filmed in open country. They needed riders who were very experienced horsemen. I first learned about the Discovery Channel commercial while at a wardrobe fitting for the movie production of *Wild Bill*. With a little prying on my part, I got the location address from one of the other actors, who at first was reluctant to offer me information since I had a reputation for having formidable horse skills.

I looked at my *Thomas Guide* and to my surprise the Discovery audition was on the way to another audition for a different production that I scheduled later that day. I decided to crash the audition and give it my best shot.

Most claimed to be expert horsemen, but I knew they couldn't ride a horse if their lives depended on it. Some couldn't mount a horse bareback let alone ride one full speed without a saddle. This I witnessed at previous auditions during the year. I was one of a few Native people in the industry who could pull off this type of horse stunt, especially bareback.

Although I am of mixed blood, Mexican and Comanche, and not a poster child for an authentic Native American look, I knew I could get the job done if given the chance. Luck was on my side that day because I was one of two people they chose to meet with the director and producer to audition our riding skills. We met a few days later at a ranch where I rode bareback for them, and I was hired on the spot since I was the better rider of the two.

We contracted for two days of location shooting on the beautiful Tejon Ranch located in the Tejon Pass off the Interstate-5 Freeway in Southern California where many Westerns were filmed due to its scenic Montana-type of view.

I had my own dressing trailer, makeup artist, and wardrobe person on the set. I was the only talent/stuntman on the set, so I got special treatment, and the supporting characters were twenty head of horses. I was outfitted in traditional Lakota plains regalia, and the horse I was to ride was a Hollywood-type Indian Paint Horse with no saddle, spurs, or even a riding crop.

There was a boss wrangler and eight wranglers (cowboys) who were chasing runaway horses all day between shots. I was trying to prove to the wranglers and the stunt coordinator that I really knew how to ride. I wanted to gain their respect because earlier that day they were standoffish and treated me as if I didn't know anything about horses... as though I were sort of a "city slicker" actor. It was a matter of time before I would prove them wrong.

I completed my two-day job in one tiring day. The following day after lunch they were going to film a cowboy chasing a herd of horses and ultimately roping one for the camera. The director asked me if I wanted to stick around to watch the filming and I agreed. Again the horses were running all over the place — because of open country. The wranglers really earned their pay on both days!

It turns out the night before the director contemplated shooting an additional stunt using me, but this time there was a great deal of danger involved. After filming the cowboy roping series they asked me if I was willing to be mounted on my Paint Horse in the middle of a herd of horses that were penned up and then released. I was to ride out of the corral, hit my ground-mark, which was a sandbag and almost impossible to see, as the horses and I were to squeeze through a gate.

The plan was to film a herd of horses from above, and then the camera would pan up to see a Native American riding in the midst of the herd. There was a high potential for danger on this stunt, because horses, like dogs, will scramble to get out, and there would be lots of bumping around with the horses fighting for position to escape confinement. If I were to get knocked off my horse I would be in serious trouble. Imagine being trampled by not one but a herd of horses in close proximity. Four iron hoofs each!

The average stuntman has six broken bones; I had already experienced one broken leg, two herniated disks, one shoulder operation, and I won't mention all the countless bumps and bruises.

I quickly got into regalia, and I was ready to mount up. Once I was in the corral and in position I knew my focus had to be laser-like with no room for error. One of the wranglers with a stereotypical Western-hick accent climbed up on the fencing and said, "Ya betta grab on ta a handful of mane and hold on. Ya don't wanna go down under them horses!" I responded with, "Believe me; if I go down, this horse is going down with me!"

The director and cameraman were sitting next to the camera, which was located on the boom high above. I was in position, and I felt the adrenaline start to kick in, the sweaty palms, and the excitement. The horses were restless, and everyone else (wranglers, crew members, and bystanders) were all waiting to see me get dumped

The author riding for Discovery Channel commercial (Donated by Bill Hatcher).

and trampled. All of a sudden I heard, "Rolling! Action!" The gate flew open, and the horses made a mad dash for the gate!

Horse flesh was all around me; my legs were getting crushed on both sides! At one point I used the horse next to me to help keep my balance when another horse overpowered mine for position and almost knocked me off. One hand tight on the horse's mane and the other controlling the rope that was makeshift reins, and we were off and running! I made my mark, the herd and I took off into the wide-open scenic country. What a feeling! It took eight wranglers the usual forty-five minutes or longer to round up the horses that were scattered.

When the horses were rounded up, the director wanted to do it one more time. This time he asked me if I could catch up to the lead horse and turn the entire herd around so the camera could take a lateral shot of me and the horses in a full run with the impressive scenery and captivating sunset filling the background. I said, "Sure, no problem. I can do that!" Then I walked over to the stunt coordinator and told him the director was crazy. There is no way I could catch up to the lead horse without spurs or a riding crop (whip).

Once again I heard "Action!" This time it was worse because the herd was a bit wiser and knew to scramble out. I have worked with movie horses many times

Bill Hatcher

The author on horseback filming on the set at Tejon Ranch (Donated by Bill Hatcher).

before and knew they get wise to what is expected from them with every take — I was ready for them.

I am sure each one of those horses was thinking, "First one out gets the first taste of freedom!" I almost got knocked off but managed to stay on by manipulating my balance by pushing off the horse next to mine. It was no longer a concern for me if I fell off. My focus was on making my little Paint Horse fly like the wind in order to catch up to the lead horse. Did this horse have it in him? If he did, I would bring it out. Did this horse really accept my friendship earlier when I blew my breath into his nostrils as my grandfather had taught me to connect with a horse? Or did this horse believe in "every man/animal for himself" and was he not going to side with me in any way?

My balance was perfect as we made the mark for the second time. Ironically, I found harmony with the horse's body rhythm as I was simultaneously kicking the heck out of him. This was not an easy feat with soft moccasins that really weren't much more than light taps to the ribs. But we were in tandem — a form of focused meditation.

By sheer fate, my horse responded to my ability as a horseman. Of course, my weighing only 155 pounds also helped. We flew as if my horse had wings. Together we passed one horse after another until we caught up with the lead horse, who bounded with the glory that freedom allowed him. The thunderous pounding hoofs shook the ground around us. The snorting of horses harmonized with a sea of long manes floating and waving through the air. A cloud of dust surrounded us, reflecting the horses' free movement in an open range. The heavy cracking of natural vegetation and the ground-pounding stride of every animal was exhilarating — I felt alive!

I managed to catch up to the lead horse and turn the herd around, and the director got his shot! My little war pony and I did it! The excitement of triumph was worth more than the money. It was an inheritance from my ancestors, the Comanche, the greatest warrior horsemen of the Southern Plains, and the Mexican *vaqueros* (cowboys) who rightfully claim to be the first cowboys of the Southwest. It was pure bliss, and I felt like it was my purpose to complete this task.

What happened next was unusual, and it made the hair on my arms shoot straight up. I could no longer hear anything although I could feel the wind blowing the two Golden Eagle feathers tied to my waist-length hair, displayed like a flag of courage. Then, all of a sudden I heard someone call out my youth name, "*Wedo*" (pronounced Weh-doe). I turned my head to my right to see six other horsemen surrounding the herd. I recognized all of them. There was my grandfather C. H. Alvarado, his two brothers Jose and Juan Alvarado, my great-uncle Pilar (the real Pecos Bill described in legends), my adopted Apache uncle Leroy Big Rope and his youngest son, my Apache brother Roylee Big Rope. All of them were in solid form riding real horses. My grandfather continued to call out my name, and then shouted, "We will help you take them back!"

I nodded my head to signal my understanding. I acknowledged the existence of these Spirit Riders, and a feeling of inner joy and love came over me. They were my family members who came from the spirit world to help me in my time of need.

What was equally amazing was their appearance played a role in supporting me as a horseman, in a sense to offer me confirmation that being a horseman was an integral part of who I am, not only in a traditional fashion, but more of a spiritual one. I was also happy to see they were still involved with horses even in the spirit world. This idea brought me a sense of joy in *knowing* I will be able to enjoy what the majestic horse can offer me not only here, but also in the afterlife.

You can only imagine how I felt: the excitement the ride offered, its danger, and on top of that the experience of having my family help me out when I was in need. I still get choked up even after all these years when I think about that event. It was truly an awesome experience that I wish everyone could have in one way or another so they can have their own truth.

All were special people in my life, and it was good to see them looking well. They were cowboys, doing what they loved the most. They were riding as Spirit Riders upon the backs of their other half, the horse that is a reflection of their true selves. When they appeared to me they were in the flesh, solid, and on real horses, saddles and all.

The seven of us drove the horse herd back to the corral, and the production crew went crazy hollering and cheering — I was given a standing ovation. They thought they were celebrating the fact that I had herded those horses on my own. They did not see the other six Spirit Riders. I thanked these Spirit Rider relatives of mine and thanked the Creator for the experience of love and knowledge that was given to me on that day.

I felt proud and thankful that my relatives came to me out of the wind, perhaps from another dimension, to share their love and skill. As I approached the wranglers

Richard Jr. and the author in 2009. Horsemanship tradition (by Erica Alaniz).

to return my little Paint Horse I said, "I hope I earned your respect on that ride. It was important to me."

When one of the wranglers walked toward me to take my horse, the boss wrangler said, "You put your own horse away." It was his way of giving me respect as a horseman. I guess he saw that I was not only able to control the herd alone, and get the shot for the director, but could also do it bareback, which takes a lot more experience.

I finally received some respect from the wranglers for that ride, and I thanked the Creator once again for allowing the experience with my family from the spirit world. I never told anyone on the set what had transpired because I knew they would not have believed me. Not that I thought anyone would believe me, but more that they would think I was not of sound mind.

Even though this type of visitation from a family member has happened to me more than once, I still wonder how they are able to manifest themselves into the physical world in solid form, as if they had never died. It is not possible at this time to offer a scientific explanation to what I witnessed.

I am not asking you, my reader, to *believe* my stories, when even people who know me want to believe me but show some doubt when I have shared these profoundly unbelievable tales. It is for you to experience personally or to come to a knowledge that there is more to life than the physical world as we know it. We are constantly being watched and guided by our spirit guides or guardian angels that are serving us as our spiritual helpers. I have come to a knowing. However, it is my truth. You are not to *believe* me. I am here to guide you to be open to your own truth that will be supported with your own experiences, which I feel can only be offered from the spirit world if you are open.

My wish is that everyone can experience a family member coming back to life after death in solid form, even if for a brief moment. It truly is very personal and spiritually fulfilling. You will come to understand that everything is possible, and there is more than what science is capable of understanding and beyond what a religion can offer. Until we can all know this truth I will cherish it and share it with whoever is willing to mentally ride side-by-side with me as I tell my story of the Spirit Riders of the Wind.

Where Is God During War?
Traumas and Lessons of War

One could or should ask where was God in 1975 when Pol Pot and his Khmer Rouge imposed their form of communism on their *own* people by slaughtering over three million Cambodians until 1979. Do you remember being entertained by the movie *The Killing Fields*? If so, you witnessed a reenactment of the Cambodian genocide.

US Army Vietnam
17th Infantry

1st Logistical Com.

1st Cavalry Divison

Where was God when the U.S. government almost brought its Native Americans to extinction with their own practice of genocide in the 1800s to further its cause for land expansion under the doctrine of Manifest Destiny? Where was God when hundreds of thousands of innocent women and children were slaughtered by Americans and North Vietnamese in Vietnam? Where was God during the Holocaust? Where is God when any form of misdeed is taking place against the innocent and those who worship Him through their faith? How can a country or group of people say God is on their side when they force their will with murderous military actions against another country or innocent defenseless humans?

In May of 1971, the war in Vietnam was going strong, and the U.S. government was drafting its nineteen-year-old sons to go halfway around the world to kill and be killed. For whatever reasons the U.S. government had for war, it was my time to sacrifice life or limb as my father did during World War II. It wouldn't be until ten years later after being discharged when I learned that communism wasn't the main reason for our military intervention in Vietnam. In reality, the war was also about controlling drugs, rubber, and other resources — specially the drug trade, which helps to finance covert CIA operations.

My extensive research brought me to a horrible realization that I took part in dehumanizing the Vietnamese people as directed by my government. This was supported by the idea that God was on our side as we fought against evil portrayed as infectious Communists in a Godless part of the world. This was the propaganda administered to us during our military training.

During my advanced infantry training part of our indoctrination included brain-washing techniques, which included the use of films to dehumanize the Vietnamese people. Our country was asking us to defend *freedom* by killing "Godless Communist vermin." I was already an experienced deer hunter, and I thought going to Vietnam would be just another hunting trip, except it would last for one year and my game would be people who were trying to hunt and kill me.

During my training, I told myself I would not fall for the propaganda. I promised myself that I was not going to subscribe to the idea that the Vietnamese were put on this planet for me to kill. If I were a true warrior then it would be warriors who I should defend myself against, not innocent civilians, even if they are families of the enemy. I compared the Vietnamese to Native Americans who were vilified in the exact same way by the U.S. government during the Indian Wars for its own political agenda. I was going to fight but only to defend myself and my friends. My battle cry was "Survive or Die."

When I talk of governments, I refer to the unknown powerful people who run governments. These are elite central bankers and corporations who profit from war by using the media, which they control, to induce fear in order to achieve a specific agenda. Many governments know that if they present an adversary as evil and threatening the people will be easily motivated to support war.

I took a weekend leave after Basic Combat Training and got married on July 10, 1971, to Rosalie, who was pregnant with our daughter Yvette. After my furlough I returned to Fort Ord, California, for Advanced Infantry Training where I met Private McFarland. McFarland seemed to be a cool guy, an ex-hippie, and also an "ex-long haired" like me. What was different about him was a presence of calmness and serenity as if he were not afraid of going to Vietnam or of even dying.

McFarland was not going to carry a rifle or take part in killing anyone even if it meant his own death. He was a conscientious objector, a one hundred percent "Jesus freak," as they were referred to in the 1970s.

The author in Camp Holloway, Plieku, Central Highlands, Vietnam 1972.

When we talked at length he seemed to have a distinctive sense of conviction. It was almost contagious, and it was the first time I truly came to understand the appeal of a religion. I was raised a Catholic, but by the time I was fourteen I was not forced to go to church. My parents gave me the choice to practice religion or not, even though they set the foundation for me as a child. I became a Christian under McFarland's influence before I was sent overseas to a distant land that held an unknown danger for me. God was on my side now, and I felt safe — or at least I thought.

In September 1971, I found myself standing on foreign soil. There was a different smell to this country, and I realized that life was no longer an absolute. The scent of this country gave the reality of death a new meaning. People were trying their hardest to make the best of life, even if they did not know if they would survive the war a week or a day, let alone an hour. I could not imagine God would allow atrocities that I witnessed to transpire in such a beautiful country.

On Christmas Day of 1971, I helped unload children from a two-and-a-half-ton military truck that had transported Vietnamese orphans and Catholic nuns to our rear base camp area in Cam Ranh Bay. Our company was assigned to feed them a healthy Christmas dinner, and I happened to be on rest time at our company rear area at the time of their arrival.

With every child I helped unload off the truck I became angrier with God and the war. I had to witness first-hand what war does to the innocent. I saw children who were missing legs and arms, a boy with only one eye, and another around the age of three, head shaved, with an opening on top of his skull — brains protruding. How could God allow this type of suffering among innocent orphans? At that instant, I changed my ideology — there was no God, and this terrible world induces greed and violence. The war was taking its toll on innocent women, children, and the elderly.

"Wars exist because God does not exist. Otherwise God would intervene," is what I thought in that moment. Even the faithful and innocent were being traumatized, punished, dehumanized, and killed. I was a witness to what humans will do to fellow human beings.

On the day I renounced Christianity, I knew if I was to survive I had to create my own luck. Every time one of my comrades was killed I would say to myself, "Better him than me." This was a statement we *all* said under our breath. The world lives on, and you will be forgotten like everyone else who was forgotten before you — I became an atheist.

On four different occasions I cheated death in Vietnam — I am not supposed to be here — but I was always spared in some mysterious way. It was as if I was not meant to die on foreign soil, as if I had someone watching over me. As an atheist how could one explain miracles?

My first escape from death occurred when I was almost decapitated but was warned by a silent voice within that told me to turn around and duck! One more inch or one split second later and I would have been headless. What a sight for my family to see once I was sent home for burial. A closed casket would have been the order of the day.

On another occasion my life was spared. By January 1972, troop levels had dropped to 156,800. My company was security for Alpha Area, the largest ammunition dump in Vietnam, with a five-mile perimeter, located in Cam Ranh. During the Easter Offensive in early April 1972, Sappers (the Viet Cong version of a U.S. Navy Seal) infiltrated our rear area, threw grenades into hootches and with AK47s shot at Americans as they were running out. This was a planned divergence to blow up Alpha Area, which they ultimately succeeded in doing. I was relieved from duty earlier that day from Alpha Area. Later that evening the first hootch they hit was next to mine. I ran outside with my M-16 to intense explosions and AK47s. Sappers were engaged and killed. After the attack, in mid-April, my unit was sent north to Plieku Province located in the Central Highlands of Vietnam to help defend against a large enemy force of the North Vietnamese Army (NVA).

The morning of April 23, 1972, the NVA launched a conventional attack on Tan Canh, which is twenty-five miles north of Kontum, and defeated 10,000 troops of the Army of South Vietnam (ARVN). Kontum was next in line to fall. After Kontum, Plieku was the next step to overtaking the American-held Camp Holloway. Tan Canh fell in one day, and although the ARVN Special Forces Ranger Units fought well and were very brave warriors — many of the regular ARVN soldiers and officers threw away their weapons and uniforms, and ran to save themselves from the onslaught of the encroaching Communists.

April 30, 1972, the U.S. combat troop level dropped to 69,000. Where there was usually a battalion (up to 1,000 men) of Americans in the area, there was only my company, Delta Company/17th Infantry Regiment/1st Logistical Command/U.S. Army Vietnam — with ARVN units, some indigenous Montagnard mountain people of Vietnam trained by American Green Berets, and Chinese mercenaries hired to defend Camp Holloway's perimeter. We were rifle security for the First Aviation, and our job was to stop two advancing NVA divisions (up to 30,000 men) who were fortified in the mountains north of Tan Canh.

During the first few days of June 1972, two NVA divisions of veteran soldiers with Russian T-54 tanks supplied earlier that year were battling in Kontum — many were dying on both sides. Plieku, located just south of Kontum, was next. My company was one of only two American Infantry units stationed at Camp Holloway. We were to face them with nowhere to go. Death was inevitable, and I understood it was only a matter of time. We were ready and waiting.

My platoon of twenty soldiers was assigned to defend a large area in the bush that should have been assigned to a full company (150 men). We were given our

Specialist 4th Class Richard Alaniz (L) & Sp4 Walker (R). Central Highlands, Plieku Province, Vietnam 1972.

orders, and we had no choice. Every man dug in and each soldier was issued six LAWs (anti-tank weapons), a case of hand grenades, two cases of M-16 ammunition, and we only had one 81mm (millimeter) mortar with cases of mortar rounds. I set the charges of the mortar rounds for long range and others for close range.

Daisy chains of M18 Claymores (anti-personal fragmentation mines) were strategically set out to our front. A daisy chain is formed when two or more Claymores are strung together to fire at the same time with a hand control clacker device. We were to face a head-on attack, and the NVA were on their way to eliminate us all. Some of our troops were scared, others were angry, but the majority of us were numb.

We were supplied with as much ammunition as could be spared. However, we did not make up enough troops to defeat the oncoming enemy to keep us alive, as we could not depend on the ARVN forces. This meant we were to hold our ground regardless of the odds, and it was going to be a slaughter for us as it was in Tan Canh a week earlier. "We are all going to die," is what some of us whispered to each other. Some of us were innocent, others were not-so-innocent. Some were scared, some indifferent. All were young — we were going to die. There would be no survivors, and the top brass was safe in helicopters or in the rear base area giving orders while nineteen-year-old boys shielded them with their lives so others would have time to evacuate. We were crassly known by everyone as "nineteen-year-old bullet stoppers."

We knew the ARVNs were weak since Tan Canh fell in one day. When we heard over the radio that Kontum was being hit hard and we were next with no plan of evacuation provided for us, a few of the guys cursed the military. Once it all sank in that we were possibly left for dead, and it was just a matter of time, fear and anger set in. No one belittled or begrudged those who expressed a little fear. We were all brothers about to share the same experience — death.

Our company was thinly spread out and no match for two NVA divisions, especially with Russian T-52 tanks at their front. I remember damning the military then, saying, "If we are going to die, we are going to die together. We are warriors, like it or not! Let's kill as many of them before they kill us all!" Of course it was a way to mask my fear.

This final battle cry momentarily gave a few of us strength, but we were soon weakened by an unwavering and unforgiving reality. Any moment our demise would be upon us. But hour after hour passed and with it, our bravery and resolve.

Mentally tortured for three days as we painstakingly waited for Kontum to fall, we counted every second, day and night, with almost no sleep, waiting for the main assault to come.

I thought about what the enemy was going to do to my body in some way to humiliate my corpse as payback for what the U.S. was doing to Vietnam. One thing I knew for sure, I was not going to let them take me alive.

Only officers are taken prisoner; enlisted men are tortured then killed after suffering a slow death — revenge is the purpose behind this. My fear was swollen with anger, and I hated all of life. I denounced God when I saw what had happened to innocent orphans, and I denounced God a second time. "Could this be God's will?" The hell with that, I thought!

All night the battle in Kontum was going strong; we could feel the concussion of bombs for three days. I could not change the immediate future, but I could go out as a warrior. I reminded myself that I was a Mexican-Comanche, a well-trained soldier and modern-day warrior. This war was not about governments or politics anymore. It was about me and the warriors coming to kill me for a cause they believed in. Although I considered myself a dead man, I felt in control of what little future I had left, and that short future involved a plan.

It was going to be like no other firefight I experienced. I pictured it in my mind over and over all night long as the rain pummeled me until I was numb. I rehearsed the scene in my mind. "Pump those mortar rounds as fast as possible until the barrel turns red-hot. Grab my M-16, one shot at a time well aimed; take out as many as possible. Piece of cake! Just like deer hunting! Throw grenades that I had spread out and placed near me. Detonate those Claymores like it was the 4th of July! Throw the NVA a party! And for the finale, use the .45 caliber pistol on the soldier who will face me eye to eye. He will know who will take his life, or I will know who will take mine!" After reciting these lines over and over, I was tired and wet from rain. I wanted it to start so it could end. Extremely angry, I no longer wanted to live — I invited death.

At the end of the third day, our radio operator got an incoming call that John Paul Vann, an ex-military man, was commanding ARVN forces, used BGM-71 TOW wire guided anti-tank missiles mounted onto *Slicks* (Huey helicopters), and along with directing 300 B-52 strikes was able to take out the Russian T-54 tanks and destroyed most of the two NVA divisions. By June 5, 1972, the advancement of the

NVA forces was temporarily halted in Kontum. We were safe for the moment — the possibility that I *might* survive the war improved.

I did not realize it at the time, but this was truly a miraculous event. John Paul Vann in reality is a hero; he was the only person left in Vietnam who could have saved my life because President Nixon was pulling combat units out trying to de-escalate the war, and the NVA were taking full advantage of the situation. They were moving in full force to take their country back and they knew we were pulling out.

On June 9, 1972, John Vann was killed when his helicopter crashed while flying in darkness. He was forty-seven. He was awarded the Distinguished Service Cross for his efforts at Tan Canh and the Presidential Medal of Freedom posthumously for achieving what no other could in Kontum.

Not too long after the battle of Kontum, some of us were surprisingly given a four-week-early out from our one-year tour of duty. Six other *grunts* (infantry men) and I were picked up in the field soon afterward and were sent back to Camp Holloway to grab our personal gear — we were going home! We were to take a *Freedom Bird*, as we called them, out of Tan Son Nhat Airport in Saigon — destination U.S.A.

Within twenty-four hours I was standing in Travis Air Force Base in California then mounted a bus heading toward San Francisco Airport. We crossed the Golden Gate Bridge, and my other comrades and I were numb and in awe of everything that had transpired in the last few days. How is it possible to be in the bush (war zone) one day and in the next day be in civilization — were we really home?

While crossing the Golden Gate Bridge I was convinced for the first time that miracles do happen. In fact they happened more than once in Vietnam. I was spared a hideous death. How was this possible? It couldn't have been an act of God, because there was no God. Could it have been because of my actions on the first day out in the bush?

My first duty was to guard an area called "point." It was a location in Cam Ranh Bay that was out in the far end of a peninsula where a two-man post was secured. We were to keep that area of the bay free from sampans. A sampan is a common means of water transportation for Vietnamese, as in a small fishing boat which could carry a Sapper close enough to shore where he could swim to land and detonate satchel charges and wreak havoc on a well-fortified area. A satchel charge is a back-pack explosive device with straps. Satchel charges were used by Sappers to sabotage inland installations or firebases. Sappers were highly trained and brave. They were the elite Viet Cong warriors and were fearless.

I would have never guessed that my first night on duty I would see action. My partner was a short-timer (a soldier at the end of his tour of duty) with an attitude. Around 1:30 a.m., I saw through my starlight scope a sampan with five occupants coming into the bay. As they were approaching I woke my partner and told him what was happening. I asked for his advice. He was more annoyed that I woke him up than anything else. His response was he didn't give a "rat's ass" what I did since he was "short" (less than a week for him to go home) and any and everything, including me, could "kiss his ass."

I stood watching through the scope and could see the sampan getting closer and closer with each minute. I had a decision to make. Were these men Viet Cong or merely some fishermen getting an early start or maybe lost? Regardless who they were I could be a hero and the first of the new guys to get a confirmed kill. Not just one kill, but five of them. According to the military, enemy or not, a kill is a kill — a body count. I would be the talk of the company, perhaps receive a medal for preventing a potential Sapper attack. My adrenaline was running wild, and the more I thought about it the more real it became that I had the lives of five human beings at my will. I pulled back the receiver of my M-60 machine gun. They were in my sights and were within kill range.

On the first day out in the field I had the power to take a life as well as be rewarded for doing so. I looked carefully in my sights, and I knew I was looking at five dead men — I hesitated. A voice within me, it was my voice but it was not me talking, was telling me to look carefully at the five individuals. What I saw was someone's father, someone's son, an uncle, or even possibly a grandfather. They were men, human beings, and I was to look at them in real life, not as in a film that dehumanized them as the military wanted me to do. In the end these men were human beings, and it was my decision.

If they were the enemy I pictured them as people who were trying to defend their land against intruders who were killing their families. I placed them in the same category as I would Native Americans trying to free their land of invaders. I did not see labels of "Communist" or any other terms that separated them from who I was. I could clearly see each of their faces and noticed they carried no weapons.

I had to take action — I was locked and loaded, and my finger was on the trigger ready to do what I must — I fired.

The noise was intense; rat-tat-tat-tat! Billowing flames reached out from the end of my barrel with every round that exited. The night came alive with thunder and white flashes. Because every third round was a red tracer I could see exactly where my rounds were hitting. I could see in the starlight scope that the people I was shooting at were falling on the deck of their boat.... Something amazing came over me; I felt alive and empowered, something greater than being a hero.

I made a decision to let them live. I managed to place rounds all around them as a warning. I don't know how they were able to turn that boat around while on their stomachs, but they did. They were spared, and I felt good about letting them live. If they were the enemy then they would live to fight on another day. If they were fishermen, it was their lucky day. From that point on I pledged I would never kill another human unless that person was shooting directly at me.

My partner didn't even blink an eye or wake up from all the gunfire. It was a typical night on the job for him. He could care less if anyone lived or died that evening. I stayed up the rest of the night, taking his shift, thinking about what happened. I was convinced there was an entity that was communicating with me. It was reasoning with silent words and mental images. It was a profound experience.

Is it possible there was a spirit looking over me? Was this thing or person here to guide me in keeping my sanity and not falling prey to being an inhumane murderer? Or was I simply in a state of delirium because of the excitement of being able to take human life? It was the beginning of an ongoing communication with the internal voice that was guiding me. I was involved in firefights after this incident but I can honestly say I never shot at anyone unless they were shooting at me or my comrades. My quest was to survive, not to kill as many Vietnamese as I could for the sake of killing. I was not blood-thirsty like most.

This experience, along with many others I faced in Vietnam, changed my life. I beat death on four different occasions while I was there — miracles do happen. Every day I live after returning from Vietnam is a day given back to me as if I had been raised from the dead. This has been my philosophy. Was it God who sent John Paul Vann? I researched years later only to find it was a "coincidental" chance that he would be at the right place and time to successfully command so that I might survive for a purpose. It was truly more than a mere coincidence, because *a lot* of coincidences put him there.

A few weeks after my friends and I left Plieku, joint forces of NVA and Viet Cong regiments overran our position and our base — my life was spared. Casualties in 1972 were 25,787 ARVNs and 851 U.S. Forces killed and 3,936 Americans wounded while battling a massive three-prong conventional attack from many divisions of joint NVA and VC forces. August 23, 1972, the last U.S. combat troops departed Vietnam. The war ended on April 30, 1975. Fifty-eight thousand-plus names are inscribed on the Vietnam Memorial Wall — luckily my name isn't there.

I feel I came out unscathed physically, mentally, and emotionally for a reason that was not by chance, but by design. It is rare I will talk of my experiences in Vietnam, and there is a three-month period I cannot account for while there. The only reason I am sharing my experience is so my reader may see how the spirit world has touched me in every aspect of my life throughout my spiritual evolution — including during war.

I was attached to Charley Co. 2nd/7th First Air Cavalry Division (Airmobile) based in Fort Hood, Texas, when I came home from Vietnam. I was assigned and ordered to train/oversee a second lieutenant and some new recruits in combat tactics as an airmobile (helicopters) infantry unit. Since they were not sending troops to Vietnam I was training these new recruits to kill for perhaps another war looming in the near future. I thought to myself, "When will it ever end?" We must learn that war at times is needless and in most cases is created to line the pockets of elite corporations.

I understand most people are not interested in serious issues. I notice that many are conditioned to focus on entertainment, perhaps as a means to keep them complacent by those who want to control how one thinks. It is a sad truth that historically many religions support war — reinforcing the concept of "Good vs. Evil."

It was not God that sent me to Vietnam; it was my government, which turned me into a product of their war machine and was responsible for the loss of many young American men and eight women. Statistically 80% of the people killed in Vietnam were innocent women, children, and elderly Vietnamese. The government calls this "collateral damage" and wants us to accept this as a byproduct of war — and we do. We forget this with every war we participate in.

A loving God never supports wars. Wars are manmade and motivated by greed, power, and control. If you perform your own research and follow the *money* you will find elite bankers and corporations profit from wars. Their motivation is not only money; it is power that they seek. The media simply uses politics and religion as an excuse to motivate people to support wars. They employ fear by suggesting that an enemy is a threat to your safety and to the welfare of the country.

I relinquished my atheistic views when my father appeared to me not long after his passing. This experience was a pivotal moment and caused me to look deeper into my experiences in Vietnam. After analysis and reflection, I concluded the spirit world does exist and for the most part it represents unconditional love for us and helps us to feel the same for our fellow human beings.

I dedicate this chapter to John Paul Vann and my fallen comrades of Delta Company 17th Infantry Regiment USARV — SSG George R. Henson of San Angelo, TX, & Sgt. Corner M. Davis of Anderson, SC, both killed on June 23, 1972; and Sp4 Robert D. McLaren of Wichita, KS, who died on June 24, 1972 — you are not forgotten — *Memorial Tribute* on last page.

Vietnam War death toll: 4,242,846 est. military and civilians, both sides.

X-Ops

A Heightened Experience with the Paranormal

(Courtesy of Jim Castle)

X-Ops Production Cast

James Castle: producer, writer, director

Scott Willmann: co-producer

Jim Marrs: author, investigative reporter

X-Ops team members:

    Laura Lee: clairvoyant psychic medium

    Karyn Reece: clairvoyant psychic medium

    Heidi Hollis: author

    Joshua Warren: author, paranormal investigator

    Brian Irish: paranormal investigator

    Ruben Uriarte: author, lecturer, MUFON director

    Nick Redfern: author, lecturer, expert on the 1947

    Roswell crash

    Richard Alaniz: author, lecturer, indigenous spiritual expert

On July 8, 1947, public information officer Lt. Walter Haut issued a press release under orders from base commander Col. William Blanchard. The newspaper headlines read, "RAAF Captures Flying Saucer on Ranch in Roswell Region." The debris recovered by sheep rancher William W. "Mac" Brazel was collected by the U.S. military from the Roswell Army Air Field under the direction of base intelligence officer Major Jesse Marcel. The following day another press release was issued from Gen. Roger Ramey declaring the incident as nothing more than a weather balloon, not a UFO sighting.

So began the saga of one of the best-known alleged UFO cover-ups in history, bringing notoriety to Roswell for years to come. Current reports of alien activity as well as other anomalies in the Roswell area were the basis of the *X-Ops* paranormal investigation production financed by the Discovery Channel in November of 2005.

Who would have known that after three years of retirement I would meet a producer by *coincidence* at a wedding reception? After a few minutes of small talk, the conversation of spirituality came up. The producer, James "Jim" Castle, was very interested in what I was doing at the time with spiritual healing and my involvement with Mescalero Apache and other indigenous shamanic practices. Jim summarized his proposal for the production of *X-Ops*, a reality program featuring eight paranormal investigators researching reports of a spirit apparition of an alien in the rehabilitation center in Roswell, New Mexico, as well as other anomalies reported at the Roswell UFO Museum.

Jim wanted me to look at the pilot treatise and offer my opinion on his program. After discussing the program I was overwhelmed when he offered me a position as one of the *X-Ops* team members to represent the perspective of indigenous spiritual healing practices. He thought it fitting that I was born in Artesia, a small town located forty-five miles south of Roswell, especially since some of my family members have admitted to experiencing one or more UFO sightings.

Jim Marrs, author of many books on conspiracy theories and other investigations about the paranormal, became our investigative reporter for the *X-Ops* team. The other team members included two technical analysts, two clairvoyant psychics, one Ufologist/crop circle expert, one author on the 1947 Roswell UFO incident, one expert on shadow people (silhouettes of frightening, dark, human-like entities), and an expert in indigenous spiritual concepts.

The purpose of the *X-Ops* team was to investigate reports of alien anomalies in Roswell, New Mexico. We had no scripts to read from or preconditioned direction.

This was to be a reality program but different from the shows that currently flood the screens with personal "drama" and "in-fighting" as the driving force to attract a viewing audience. This production was to take place on actual locations of the reports with no reenactments. We were all excited and willing to uncover anything that we might find or go home empty-handed.

Through Laura Lee and Karyn Reece, both psychic mediums, I learned about the many levels of psychic consciousness and how everyone has the ability to channel one's own psyche, if we are open. Remember when you were thinking of an individual and all of a sudden that person called you on the phone or appeared at your front door? This is a psychic event. However, we use words like "coincidence" or "gut feeling" to rationalize or make sense of the experience.

Roswell Army Air Field — Walker Field

After leaving our headquarters in San Bernardino, California, the X-Ops team landed at Walker Field, previously known as Roswell Army Air Field. Located on this former military air field is Hangar 84 where allegedly one live alien and two dead ones were transported by a government recovery team immediately after the 1947 UFO crash. Currently, there is a rehabilitation center located where the military hospital once stood. And in this hospital, alleged autopsies were performed on two dead aliens and exploratory surgery was performed on the live alien.

The X-Ops team members were excited to begin our four-day investigation in Roswell as we were waiting for official X-Ops vehicles to pick us up at Walker Field. This historic airport with the longest landing strip in the United States was home to the Enola Gay, the B-29 bomber piloted by Brig. General Paul Tibbets (USAF Ret.) and his crew. The Enola Gay was the bomber that carried and dropped the first atomic bomb for combat purposes at exactly 09:15 on August 6, 1945, over Hiroshima, Japan. Upon their return to Tinian Island in the Marianas chain, General Carl A. Spaatz decorated Paul Tibbets with the Distinguished Service Cross, and his crew members were given Air Medals for their role in altering the history of the world.

Roswell Rehabilitation Center

After checking into our hotel, the X-Ops team set out for a visit to the Roswell Rehabilitation Center. Jim Marrs, working as an investigative reporter, accidentally uncovered reports of an alien spirit manifestation centralized in one specific area of the rehabilitation center. He was looking for an old hospital as a shoot location for another program he was working on. The employees admitted to the sightings when he interviewed them for information about the building. He reported his findings to our producer, Jim Castle, and both felt it would be an interesting investigation.

Our job as *X-Ops* investigators was to interview various individuals, record data with scientific devices, and use the expertise of each member in their specific field to draw a conclusion as to whether an alien spirit existed in the rehabilitation center. Because of the diverse expertise of each team member, we were able to approach this endeavor from many fronts to decipher data from different perspectives and disciplines.

As we were being filmed in real time we had carte blanche to say what we wanted, positive or negative. The idea was for everything to occur as if the viewer were conducting the investigation along with us. If we found something, we would have real-time proof of what we were investigating. If nothing was found, we had to be satisfied with the results, just as any researcher or investigator must be satisfied.

The premise and format of the investigation were approved by the Discovery Channel, who oversaw it daily, and financed it with a $300,000 budget. What was amazing about this production was there were no reenactments using professional actors. The only digital imaging used was to simulate the 1947 UFO crash in order to depict the sequence of events for the audience.

Upon entering the rehabilitation center, our two psychics received confirmation of human spirits present in the center. Many overzealous individuals would even say the facility was haunted. The old military hospital was torn down years ago and replaced with the rehabilitation center. Laura and Karyn described the spirits as military personnel who had expired in the former hospital. We had a strong suspicion the corridor area where the alien spirit was reportedly seen is the exact area where the former surgical room was located. To confirm this and present it to our viewers, a superimposed layout of the old and new floor plans of the sighting location within the hospital was shown.

In the director's cut of *X-Ops*, the viewer can see anomalous orbs that flew rampantly around one room. Orbs are small round balls of suspended light energy, which are residue of a spirit's energy. They are not always visible to the naked eye. The orbs were caught on film using infrared and thermal cameras and other scientific devices. One can actually see the orbs passing through the bodies of our psychics who were simultaneously describing what they were seeing and feeling.

During an equipment maintenance break, the *X-Ops* team entered a room and decided to turn off the lights and perform a meditation to see if our psychics could contact the alien spirit who was allegedly haunting the area. Laura led our team in a breathing exercise, and after we were in deep meditation she opened a portal and invited the entity.

Brian Irish reported feeling something touch and then pass through him. The psychics identified the anomaly as the alien spirit. Soon afterward, four other *X-Ops* team members reported they were feeling the entity pass through their body with a cold static sensation. Laura and Karyn then proceeded to converse with the entity telepathically. It revealed its experience while under the scalpel of medical personnel trying to perform vivisection without anesthesia.

In 1947 doctors were using ether as an anesthesia, which was not effective for the alien as it made him sick. The surgery continued anyway since it was a once-in-a-lifetime research opportunity. The alien reported he died due to the invasive trauma.

According to our psychics, the entity communicated with us in order to tell his story and bring closure. The alien stated one U.S. military airplane and another alien aircraft chased his craft. After much shooting and chasing, the alien's craft malfunctioned, crashed, and was witnessed by the rancher, Mac Brazel. Mr. Brazel immediately reported the crash to the local sheriff. Mr. Brazel was directed by military authorities to stay silent about the incident. Long after his death, Mr. Brazel's family admitted he was in constant fear for their safety because of the threats made by the military.

The alien said he was captured and taken to a holding area, known as Hangar 84, and was inspected and probed by military authorities. It was confirmed on the last day of our investigation when we had a séance at Hangar 84.

During interviews, employees of the rehabilitation center reported an alien haunting that had been occurring for over forty years. One nurse said her mother, who worked there years before, along with other co-workers, encountered this alien back then. Other interviewees reported strange things were always going on in that particular corridor, and one even admitted, "You couldn't pay me enough money to go back there."

Laura and Karyn were interviewed on camera and presented parts of what the alien revealed during our meditation. It was late, around 3:30 a.m., and we decided to leave various cameras stationed in specific areas to record any forms of paranormal activity during the rest of the night. When the crew collected the cameras and reviewed them the following morning, they found various anomalies that offer proof of paranormal activity present in the rehabilitation center in Roswell. All of the anomalies that were captured on film are included in the director's cut of *X-Ops*.

Roswell UFO Museum

Day Two of our investigation took place in the Roswell UFO Museum and Research Center. The curator of the museum, Julie Shuster, is the daughter of Walter Haut, the museum's co-founder. Walter died in 2005 and was the public information officer who issued the press release of the UFO crash in Roswell in 1947. He was given orders from base commander Col. William Blanchard to release the findings to the press only to rescind the information the following day.

Walter Haut was one of many military personnel who knew the truth of the 1947 crash and was compelled to share information as well as other reports by creating the Roswell UFO Museum. He will be known in history as a dedicated individual who defied authority to get information to the public in an effort to expose the truth about extraterrestrial life forms.

Without a doubt this was a day that forever changed my perspective on extraterrestrials (ETs) and other anomalies concerning multidimensional beings. You may wonder, "How can Richard ask me to believe what he experienced when he lectures against belief systems?" I cannot and would not ask you to *believe* me. All I can hope for is your patience and your willingness to be open to an experience of your own, if that is your Karmonic Experience.

The museum contains various exhibits and displays. Most notable is a large array of historical items and information concerning the alleged UFO crash in 1947.

Roswell UFO Museum, founded in 1991. (Courtesy of Julie Shuster, Director)

Although the museum attracts a large number of tourists, it also houses an extensive research center for those seriously interested in Ufology.

I wandered around the museum while listening to the various interviews conducted by other team members. As I was walking upstairs I felt a cold chill and smelled cigarette smoke. I ran upstairs and interrupted one of the interviews, asking if anyone was smoking. No one was smoking, and the museum employees stated that smoking was never allowed in the building.

Running back down the stairs I wanted to see if anyone on the ground floor was smoking. I remembered from my previous experiences that cigarette smoke is a sign of the presence of a spirit. I found Laura and Karyn in the lobby and without explanation I asked them to follow me upstairs. I ignored the cameraman who asked if he should come too because at this moment, I was not concerned with making a television program; it was about confirming my own experience.

As we walked upstairs I said nothing about my experience. I simply moved up slowly until Karyn said she was seeing the spirit of a priest standing in the hallway as we reached the top of the stairs. They simultaneously reported there was an extra-terrestrial that walked off and vanished after seeing us at the top of the stairs. I learned later a priest and other people died there in a fire years before.

The psychics mentioned this was the same alien who revealed itself to them at different times and areas of the museum. Karyn told us when she was washing her hands in the restroom earlier in the day she saw him in the mirror. She reported, "He raised his head quickly and then disappeared." I remembered thinking this would have been a weird experience, especially looking casually into a mirror, not expecting to see any other image but your own. I would have certainly been spooked!

After the interviews our team continued the investigation using scientific instruments to gather data. This included thermal readings devices, electromagnetic field (EMF) readers, and an apparatus to record potential surge readings. I was using the EMF device that detects any electromagnetic field within the museum. When I placed it near a cell phone or electrical wall circuit it would emit a medium-pitched tone, and an array of red lights would flash as indicators on the meter.

I was determined to cover every inch of the museum. All of a sudden I received Induced Knowledge from my spirit guide. I was compelled to move ten feet over to my right. When I did, to my surprise the electromagnetic meter lit up and sounded off.

I looked around to double- and triple-check if there was an electrical socket nearby. There was none. There was only an aluminum frame with an advertisement banner made of cloth covering it.

After I made sure there was nothing capable of setting my meter off I called out to the other team members. As soon as they reached me, all of their instruments and meters lit up and sounded off. In the *X-Ops* episode you can actually see and hear our instruments detecting a presence. As we collected data our meters were going nuts.

Heidi Hollis was the first to report feeling a tingling sensation on her arm. Everyone placed their arms and hands over her hand and felt the same tingling that she described. At first I could not feel anything because I was holding my hand too high. Once I placed my hand lower, I could feel it!

We were collecting data and were amazed by what we were experiencing. Not knowing what we found, I called out for someone to summon our two psychics to give us confirmation. When Laura and Karyn both walked up to us, they smiled and in unison said, "It's the little alien."

Laura continued, "This is the same alien that we have been seeing all day. He is excited this is happening. Does anyone feel anything?"

We all said, "Yes!"

Then Laura said, "He is moving rapidly back and forth and at times going right through you." She explained he was a multidimensional being and was bouncing rapidly around us. She took the opportunity to ask him if he would reveal himself to us, but he did not comply.

I was amazed. I could not see the entity but I could feel him with my hand and as he was passing through me. The only way I can describe it is as a sensation of putting your hand in front of a TV screen and into a freezer at the same time. It felt cold yet there was a static-like sensation. It felt so strange, especially when it seemed to go right though my body. The feeling was intense!

All the instruments were surging — reading bursts of energy. We were all perplexed. I was then compelled to offer this entity a traditional Native American song. I was being directed by my spirit guide so I could have a positive and loving connection with this entity. The song is called "The Beautiful Way." It is not an Apache medicine song but a blessing song designed to connect to other beings.

I asked one of the crew members to get my jacket, which held my rattle. I placed a small eagle feather in my left hand and held it in front of me to bless the entity while singing the song — he was all around me.

As I sang the second verse I felt a strong surge of love. It was like being hugged by your grandmother, who has unconditional love for you, but multiplied by one hundred. I was overwhelmed with so much love that I had to stop singing. I looked over to the psychics as I placed my left hand over my chest and asked, "He is a loving being, isn't he?"

Laura answered with, "Yes he is very loving. He says he likes the rhythm of the song you are singing and feels very connected to you." I walked away in order to compose myself. I sat down and watched the team continue to gather data. I was compelled again by my spirit guide to go back and finish the song.

I walked back to the circle, but this time I closed my eyes as I sang and focused. Everyone stood back and watched. His image came into my mind's eye. He was very small in stature with long arms, a large head, large almond-shaped eyes with eyelids, and a pinkish skin color. He was not gray with the large black eyes as typically reported by those who have had abduction encounters.

He was a benevolent being and was interacting with me in a spiritual sense. I held my hand in front of me and felt him moving around and through me very rapidly. The psychics said he was joyous for the connection we were making with each other. At one point he went through Brian Irish who was standing to my left, and Brian had to grab my arm to gain his balance as if he could have been knocked over by the surge of energy, which was captured on camera. It was an amazing encounter and an incredible experience.

When I finished my song I told everyone to put down their instruments so we could form a circle with our hands in order to offer this entity our love. This I felt was just as important as collecting data for our investigation. This was real, and we were grateful to be there.

We each asked the entity a question. According to Julie, the museum curator, a display map of the U.S. located on a wall lit up when Karyn asked her question and when I asked mine. She reported the map doesn't have that many lights, but when our questions were asked, it was completely covered with light; she said she would have thought that impossible had she not seen it for herself.

After our questions, the entity was communicating with our psychics telepathically, telling them its reason for being there at the museum. It also foretold events that were to take place in the future. I will not share what the entity said at this time due to the contents of that information. I doubt you would "believe" me anyway. I feel when the time is right many will reveal information given to those who are supposed to share it. When that time comes, the world will be astonished by the information that many hold.

I was compelled to ask its name. As soon as I asked Karyn to ask him, I was guided or directed to look over to a soda machine that was close by. The large "Coca-Cola" logo stood out and the initials "C. C." came to my mind. Its name was "C. C." I yelled out, "C. C. is what he wants us to call him." Karyn confirmed this. I still wonder if "C. C." read my mind when I looked at the large letters. Regardless of the reason, we all decided to refer to the alien entity by those initials.

We returned to the museum lobby where we debriefed our alien encounter. James Castle, our producer, revealed that his hand-held camera was vibrating and shaking while he was taping. I remember when he alerted me to this, and I reached over to feel the camera. It was vibrating vigorously and for a long duration.

Even our technical researchers were astounded by what just had transpired in the museum. I suddenly realized what my true purpose was during the investigation. I finally understood that it was important for me to extend myself further. I needed to be alone with the alien to offer this benevolent being a medicine song.

I told Jim Castle I wanted to offer "C. C." another song but without any audio recording or cameras. I was to be by myself with this being. He agreed and said he would give me privacy.

I walked back to the darkened rear area of the museum where we had the encounter and after blessing the area I began my song using my rattle. I could feel "C. C." there with me, and again he was interacting with me by moving around and through me. I felt a very strong connection with him but this time it was very personal. I could envision him in my mind, and I was not afraid. It was a very loving encounter that I wish everyone could experience.

It was two o'clock in the morning, and our work day at the museum was over. We drove back to our hotel; I was exhausted and climbed into bed. As I was dozing off I felt a presence in my room. Although I have had experiences with spirits, I sensed this was different. I chose to ignore it and tried to fall asleep. I suddenly opened my eyes, and again I could feel the presence of someone. This time the feeling was stronger. I thought to myself, "No problem. I know I am protected by my spirit guide."

I communicated with the being with my thoughts: "I know you are here, but I have had enough for one day and I need to sleep!" Then I felt as if a child were walking at the foot of my bed making its way toward me. It felt eerie at first. But then I turned around to look again where I felt the movement — but I saw nothing.

As I was trying to sleep I felt something walking closer, stopping at my lower back. I was lying on my right side at the right edge of the bed so there was plenty of room behind me. I focused and saw in my mind that "C. C." was standing behind me. I turned, looked at him, and we began to communicate telepathically. What an experience!

I feel that telepathy is the greatest means of communication because sometimes spoken words are not as descriptive as a completed thought. This was confirmed as I looked at him straight on. After a short period I told him with my mind, "I am not interested at this time; I don't have enough information yet."

I could still feel him at my back, but I was exhausted, and I had a 5:30 a.m. call time to shoot in a new location. I knew he wasn't there to hurt me. What was more important was to stay in control of any situation pertaining to the paranormal. In this case everything was new to me; I had to stay focused.

In hindsight, perhaps I should have communicated longer with him to learn more about the purpose of our connection. It is not every day that one has this type of experience. However, I always go with my instincts and feel I will be better prepared in the future if I have another encounter with him or some other extraterrestrial entity. As a result of my newfound experience and further research, I have more knowledge now. I am more open to new experiences.

The next morning I went downstairs and saw Laura and Karyn in the lobby of the hotel sipping their morning coffee. I walked up to them with my arms folded and without offering a greeting. I asked, "Who was in my room last night?" They both looked at one another and laughed because of the look on my face and my bloodshot eyes.

"C. C. was with you. But don't worry... we told you he is a benevolent being. Anyway your spirit guide was there with you too," said Laura.

"I know he is benevolent, but why did he come to visit me?" I asked.

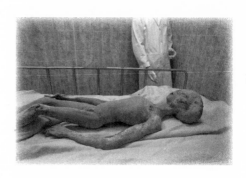

Replica of Alien found at crash site (UFO Museum). (Courtesy of Julie Shuster, Director).

Karyn responded with, "He felt connected to you and wanted to communicate with you."

"Yeah, I guess I knew that, but I was really tired. I was in no mood, so I told him that I didn't have enough information to deal with him," I snapped back.

They laughed and Karyn said that "C. C." had visited both of them as well. It turns out "C. C." was just as impressed with the three of us as we were with him.

What an experience! This was right up there with all the spirit visitations and paranormal encounters I have had. It was on another level for me, and I felt it was the beginning of something that has continued to this day. We always have to remember not to jump into any experience unprepared. Fear should be kept in check and most of all control is important because it is the key to dealing with the unknown or supernatural.

The photo above shows a display in the museum that depicts an autopsy performed by medical personnel on one of the alleged aliens found at the 1947 crash site. Notice the similarities and differences between the model and the human physical form. This alien has only four fingers and no thumb. It has no ears other than small holes on the sides of its head. The large eyes have lids like a human's, but the nose and mouth are much smaller. The head is larger and the arms are longer. There is no representation of genitalia.

Séance at Hangar 84

Hangar 84, located at the Roswell Air Base, is the metal building that allegedly housed the 1947 UFO debris, two dead aliens, and one captured living alien. The hangar was considerably large and empty, and looked as if it had not been used in many years. There were various rooms that were connected to the hangar, perhaps used as offices by former military personnel.

The *X-Ops* team was planning a séance for that evening to try to communicate with human spirits and any other multidimensional entities that may have been present. This was a new experience for me. I knew enough not to toy with this type of paranormal activity without an experienced medium to control any negative encounters. This is why I caution people not to use Ouija boards for fun or curiosity. When individuals innocently "play" this "game," there is a tendency to open portals that allow various multidimensional beings to enter your environment. The "players" may not understand that some of these beings are not friendly, and at times are demonic.

A portal is a gateway to multidimensional worlds. This is how spirits or multidimensional beings can enter our world on their own or by invitation from someone in this world. When attempting to open a portal, one should perform a protection blessing to provide a deterrent for negative beings. Once a negative being is in your midst, you will probably not be able to rid yourself of this being without professional support. My advice is not to pursue this type of experience unless you are a very spiritually evolved individual with a great deal of knowledge.

The day before the séance I was instructed by my spirit guide to give a protection blessing for the *X-Ops* team. But I wanted it to be private and controlled. I allowed the presence of our psychics and no one else because I felt the women were going to offer support and protection to the others in case we had to face any negative presence that might have appeared during the séance.

We were wandering around inspecting various rooms near the hangar. Some were well lit, and others were extremely dark. Joshua Warren, our lead scientific team member, reported later that he did not have a "good feeling" when he was investigating one of the rooms.

I walked into one room and found Laura, Karyn, and Heidi discussing their feelings about what was to transpire during the séance. There was an adjacent room that was dark, and I was compelled to perform a protection blessing inside that room. I invited the three women to come with me if they felt they needed protection.

I was not sure if they would follow me, because I didn't know if they doubted my abilities as a spiritualist. I meditated for a short period, and when I opened my eyes I could see them standing in front of me in a semicircle. I surrounded us in the White Light of Divinity and asked for protection against any and all negative spirits or multidimensional beings that we were to encounter during our visit in the hangar.

I started chanting, and I could see that Laura was going into a trancelike state. Her upper body was mildly shaking, in a rhythmical sense, while her feet remained still, almost in a hypnotic trance fashion.

The chant was powerful, and I felt the presence of my spirit guide as well as other loving spirits. With each verse of the chant I could see the three women were very focused and involved. Although it was dark there was a faint illumination that seemed to intensify as I proceeded. I could feel the support of the women who supplied me with energy to perform the protection that we all knew we would need.

When I finished, Laura smiled and said that my spirit guide, my father, and my grandmother were standing next to me. Everyone felt refreshed, and we were in a state of love and inner peace. It was time to go in the main area of Hangar 84 to begin our séance — I felt protected.

The airplane hangar was very spacious and dark. There was a large round table with eight chairs placed in the middle of the hangar. Four candles were the only source of light and were arranged on top of the table to represent the four directions. Laura guided each person, who was present for the blessing I gave, to sit in a chair directly across from one another in front of a white candle. The other four team members were seated between people who had a candle in front of them.

Everyone was briefed on how to react if they felt any form of negative presence within them. The cameras were filming in candlelight, ready to shoot anything of interest or unusual. We were ready. Laura began with an opening affirmation to open a portal and then guided us in a brief meditation.

Laura asked, "Did you guys hear that 'haaaaaa' sound that surrounded all of us?" We did. It sounded like an exhale that filled the room. I truly feel it was a negative spirit mimicking me because I use such a dynamic breathing technique when I meditate, but it was more intense. The audio technician later confirmed that he captured the anomalous sound on tape. That same eerie feeling still encompasses me whenever I watch the director's version DVD.

Karyn then acknowledged the spirit of Mac Brazel, the rancher who found the crash site, was present, giving information to her and Laura. Brazel confirmed what he found on the ranch was an actual UFO, two dead aliens, and one who was attempting to escape. He reported that he was detained four to five days, harassed by the government, and was told not to mention anything about what he had witnessed. Along with Brazel, there was another spirit of a politician/legislator who also gave us information as to how he was forbidden by the government to release files pertaining to the Roswell crash to the public. The spirit was telling our psychics that the files were hidden in a brown box housed in a secret underground room beneath the White House. The files were labeled with an innocuous and misleading title.

I feel the information given to us during the séance was highly controversial and should have been edited out of the pilot episode. We already knew we were being followed by some form of government agency since we actually watched them observing us at a distance, and it was confirmed when we received information from these spirits to "be careful because you are being watched." It was very interesting to hear communication from the spirits that confirmed the information given to us by Nick Redfern, our team expert on the Roswell UFO story.

At this point, Karyn stated we were surrounded by different kinds of entities. We heard very strange noises coming from within the hangar. At times it sounded like someone was walking softly on the roof, and at other times there were loud "clanging" noises as if someone was hitting the sides of the hangar. There was no wind outside, and everyone, including the security guard, was inside the hangar. We were perplexed as to where the noises were coming from and who or what was making them. Although I was without fear it was exceptionally eerie!

Ironically, Laura, who had many previous experiences with spirits, was a bit frightened by what was happening. On camera as her eyes opened very wide she stated in a low voice, "I almost crapped in my pants!" I guess that was her way of saying she was moved by what was happening. In fact everyone present was in awe of what was transpiring.

As I write this, I now feel that many entities were present in the hangar toying with us and doing a good job of scaring some. However, at the time I was not convinced and had to find out for myself. I got up from my chair and took a small flashlight that Brian handed me. I walked into the darkness in the direction of the clanging noises. There was nothing that I could see. No people, no pigeons, no rats... nothing that would make sense. When I think back, none of the animals I suspected would have been able to create a loud clanging sound. I truly didn't know what to expect. Unbeknownst to me, one of the cameramen followed me and captured my solo venture on film.

I didn't want to interrupt the communication Karyn was having with the spirits of Brazel and the politician, but while they were communicating, I saw in my mind a motionless alien lying on a gurney toward the back of the hangar. It was as if the spirit of the alien wanted me to see where his corpse was located. I couldn't say anything at the time, but I felt the various extraterrestrial spirit entities were communicating with me with mental images.

A few moments later, in my mind I visualized an alien running back and forth to my left near a metal wall around forty feet away from us. I was wondering why he was doing this and why I visualized him. I later learned he was showing me that he was the spirit of the alien trying to get away when they brought him to the hangar as a captive in 1947.

The other team members decided to investigate the noises further. Joshua Warren stated he was reading a very cold temperature on his thermal device, which happened to be located at the exact spot where I envisioned the alien on the gurney. When I walked over to Joshua, I felt a chill that was at least well over ten degrees cooler than the hangar. I reported my vision of the gurney to all of them at that time.

My spirit guide directed me to walk over to my left where I thought I had seen the other alien running against the wall, and there I found a chain that was flush against the metal wall and I rattled it. It was the exact sound that we were hearing earlier when I walked over in the dark with the flashlight. Strange occurrences were happening — we have it all on film — it was truly haunted with paranormal activity.

The DVD of the program shows Joshua's device suddenly turning off on its own when he and a cameraman were investigating another area of the hangar. We also see an anomalous object fly over our heads during the séance. It had a light, misty texture, and a long extended shape. It is difficult for me to describe in detail without your seeing the episode for yourself; however the DVD shows the object in real time and in slow motion. I was in awe of the activity taking place around us; we were all truly amazed by what we were experiencing.

Another interesting event occurred during our séance, which was also captured on film. Tim Keeler, one of the crew members, became suddenly ill, first falling onto his knees and then on his back. It was as if he was being attacked by something. He later reported he felt nauseous and faint as if something was overtaking him.

There was no doubt in my mind that Hangar 84 was haunted by spirits and multidimensional entities on this night, and probably other nights as well. We left with yet another experience to support our hypothesis that the government tried to cover up the Roswell UFO crash of 1947.

The DVD I keep mentioning was never actually distributed to a wide audience. After financing the *X-Ops* project with $300,000, the Discovery Channel executives suddenly refused to release it. Our producer, Jim Castle, was unable to contact the Discovery Channel producers who were working with us every day of the production. The producers were either doing their best to avoid Jim, or the people he was talking with weren't providing him with legitimate reasons for stalling the release. The film was indefinitely put "on hold," and the final project was dropped even after a large public protest with phone calls and emails against the Discovery Channel for not releasing *X-Ops*.

I intuitively feel, along with the other psychics, there were outside forces that did not want this film to be released. We as a team found what we were looking for, and the way we presented our findings was totally different from other films previously produced about ETs.

Most film productions rely on re-creations of a given storyline, leaving enough room for scrutiny. This element of doubt thereby taints most accounts of the paranormal as "entertainment." The *X-Ops* project placed the viewer in the midst of the team members, enabling anyone in the audience to experience what we experienced. The only reenactment technology used was the animation of the UFO crash and the alien that was viewed by the witnesses at the rehabilitation center. Everything else that was filmed is what actually happened, in real time. Of course skeptics could argue that we were acting in order to sell the idea of a paranormal event to our viewers, but scientific equipment doesn't lie. Thus, the only way to come to a truth is to experience it for yourself — I don't expect you to *believe*.

I remember I mentioned to our producer, Jim, not to include sensitive issues concerning the government. He felt it was an important part of the production and included this controversial footage anyway. I had a feeling there were going to be problems with its release, and *X-Ops* may not be available to the general public. Whether or not *X-Ops* will ever be released is irrelevant. This is an experience I will never forget, one that continues to play an integral part of my spiritual journey. And the experience didn't end in Hangar 84.

I had yet another incident when Tim Keeler, the crew member who fell ill during our séance, was driving Laura and me back to Los Angeles from our *X-Ops* headquarters in San Bernardino. I was sitting in the back seat, and Laura was in the passenger's side. Both back windows were halfway open as we were on the freeway.

While we were discussing the events of the séance, a butterfly flew into the window, circled my head, then landed on my left shoulder. I was surprised because an insect had never casually landed on my body while traveling at 70 miles an hour in a car!

Laura said, "Do you smell that?"

Tim said, "Yeah. It smells like burning sage." Suddenly the butterfly flew out the same window it had entered. In my mind I knew this was a message from the spirit world. I knew what I had to say to them both.

My advice to each was to bless their homes, to light a white candle and say these words as they were burning sage or incense: "I surround myself and this home in the White Light of Divinity. I do not allow any evil spirits or negative multidimensional beings to enter this home. I only allow loving spirits and my spirit guide to enter in the name of the Creator and/or Jesus Christ." I told them about the butterfly and the fact that the spirit world uses animals or insects as messengers to give us knowledge and/or guidance.

Following my own advice, I blessed my home, my studio, and my mother's house to protect my family from any entities that may have followed me home from the events of the séance and perhaps the other paranormal experiences I had with *X-Ops* while in Roswell.

A few years later, the city of Roswell sponsored their annual UFO event where researchers and speakers present various subjects of extraterrestrial phenomena. The *X-Ops* team was invited to present our DVD for the first time to the public. Since Jim Castle and team member Ruben Uriarte were going to speak and present the DVD, I felt it was not necessary for me to attend. I decided instead to spend time on a horse ride with nine other friends and family members, ironically about 70 miles southwest of Roswell, and on the last day of the UFO festivities, Monday, July 8, 2007; a very special experience was given to me.

While we were riding the territory outside of Hope, New Mexico, in the beautiful scenic upper desert, a deer jumped out of a large arroyo. The other riders were in awe as they witnessed this. I anticipated the deer would head toward a specific hill. As I was looking at the top of the hill, I noticed a brilliant silver metallic object in the sky above it. One of the cowboys yelled out, "Hey! Look at that bright thing in the sky!"

As I was observing it, I also summoned others to look up, but they didn't pay attention because they were distracted by the deer. The shiny craft was traveling in a northeastern direction, toward Roswell. It was moving very slowly, and less than a minute later, it disappeared. It was noon, and there were no clouds in the sky. I wondered, "How could a craft vanish into thin air?" But then I already knew what I was seeing.

I turned to the other cowboy who had seen it and asked him, "So what do you think it was?"

He answered, "I think that was a UFO. I believe in them."

Then I said, "That is exactly what we saw."

The shape of the craft, the texture and brilliant color, its close proximity to us, and its vanishing in daylight were confirmation for me that it was truly what is described as a UFO.

The entire *X-Ops* investigation was a life-changing experience for me, confirming that extraterrestrials do exist. People from around the world continue to report UFO sightings, yet the general public does not give any value to the reports. Is it too frightening to think extraterrestrial life forms exist? Would it cause panic? Would our religions be affected by the existence of ETs? Would people be upset with their governments for covering up the truth?

Today scientists are searching the skies for extraterrestrial communication through radio astronomy that studies celestial objects at radio frequencies. The Drake Equation, devised by Frank Drake in 1961, is used to estimate possible extraterrestrial civilizations in our galaxy. On August 15, 1977, astronomer Jerry R. Ehman, PhD, documented a "strong narrowband radio signal" from outer space while working on the SETI project. One must ask why hundreds of thousands of dollars are financing this type of research if the government officially proclaims that ETs don't exist.

The truth is coming to us, and in time all will know what I and others know about the extraterrestrial phenomenon. I feel there is a historical connection between benevolent extraterrestrials and spirituality. My wish is that you may have your own experience in order to reach a truth. In doing so, we may find our connection as humans to multidimensional beings, and the role they have and will continue to play in our existence.

PART III

THE PROBLEM WITH BELIEF SYSTEMS

AND HOW TO MOVE BEYOND

Religion vs. Spirituality

"All religious belief is a function of nonrational faith. And faith, by its very
definition, tends to be impervious to intellectual argument or academic criticism."

JON KRAKAUER, *UNDER THE BANNER OF HEAVEN*

For centuries many cultures have adopted and organized their own concepts of spirituality and its relationship to religion. This is done to address the mystery of man's
existence on Earth in order to satisfy the many questions concerning the purpose
of life. However, in a current movement toward spirituality, spirituality is defined as
a deeper, more meaningful, and broader expression than that of previous religious
formalities. There is a *new* birth of spiritual consciousness.

Some researchers believe the historical framework of organized religious practice
included ritual, mythology, animism, and a common theme, the promise of ever-
lasting life for one's soul and the fear of reprisal or damnation if one does not
follow its doctrine.

Historically religion was to provide economic and social structure to societies
with varied cultures and beliefs since most were made up of different tribes. This
allowed a central authority to dictate social structures such as keeping the peace,
taxation, and other services to a given society, while that authority played a dual role
as rulers and spiritual leaders. By organizing a common religion the populace can
bond together in a familiar and customary faith.

As religions prospered with the invention of the printing press in the fifteenth
century, widespread religious wars broke out as churches competed for world domi-
nance. With time, new religious movements developed from existing religions, which
intensified the competition for power over the centuries.

Throughout history, humans have used Holy Scripture as a tool to substantiate their reasons for waging holy wars. In actuality these wars were responsible for the deaths of countless innocent people in the name of God with the concept of "Good vs. Evil" as their justification. Warring nations each believed God was on their side, and they were merely following His will against evil. Gaining land and natural resources upon the defeat of an *evil* enemy made for a very convenient and profitable reason to make war.

In the twenty-first century, people are discovering there is more to spirituality than just sets of rules that were written over two thousand years ago. Did God only talk to a few? Do we and did we all have the capability to access awareness through spiritual consciousness? Could it be we choose not to listen to anything outside of tenacious religious ideologies?

Mine is but one perspective that will help you understand how, why, and when a connection with the spirit world may come to you. Our total collective consciousness, not only on our planet but also within the entire universe, is the makeup of what "God is." No one can prove this scientifically, but it is reasonable to feel that "God," if He/She/It has to be represented as an individual entity, remains anonymous and is not responsible for the atrocities that we bring upon ourselves. The "will" of God is nonexistent, contrary to the tenets of current religious philosophies. It is the will of mankind that we witness.

Some people will seek religion but will not be moved by or know anything about the inner self. Others will advance by knowing there is something more than organized religion and will find themselves on a quest toward a higher spiritual awareness. This may come to them at an early age or later in life, usually when experiencing an epiphany of a spiritual nature. They then become spiritually conscious of the events that take place in their lives, feel the presence of something more than themselves, and eventually experience awareness unlike before. This will lead most to investigate further, in search of the truth outside of religion or science. It is always healthy to question what we believe in. This is the purpose of evolving to our highest potential.

Throughout this book, I paint an ideological picture using the concepts of unconditional love, spirit consciousness, Induced Knowledge, Divine Intervention, Spiritual Webbing, and the supernatural. These, and other related topics, will enhance what you may already know or will enlighten you to the possibility of newfound knowledge — all of which can only be received if you open your mind to other possibilities outside of your current belief. If you are moved by the ideas or words within this book, you may be influenced to do so by guides who are directing you to a higher spiritual consciousness.

"The spirit world is alive and well," say a few who have experienced it and wish to share their knowledge with the world. Yet others say it is impossible to have experienced what was not written in Holy Scriptures, and must therefore be of Satan.

My personal experiences have directed me to feel that the word "Satan" and the concept of demons are mythological representations created to induce fear. If those in power can create archetypes and inject fear into the people, then they can control the people. Is damnation waiting for those who will not be controlled? Is there such a thing as Hell? According to Bishop John Spong, of Newark, New Jersey, "Hell is an invention of the church to control people with fear."

Do Satan and evil demons really exist, or are we associating their existence with every irresponsible act that we have performed so as not to be held accountable for our actions? If I am born on some remote island and no one tells me about Jesus or Mohammad before I die, will I go to Hell?

All of these are valid questions and the mysteries of life are the mainstay of spiritual philosophy for each person in each generation. The desire to seek a higher form of existence is within every human being, but it is *free will* that allows us to ignore the desire or to succumb to prepackaged rules of organized religion.

Religions promote Hell because it is the residence of the Devil. And the Devil, the great beast that evolved throughout time, is professed to be the greatest enemy of humankind. A more frightening idea is we will journey to Hell as punishment for not being consistent in following the word of God — damnation awaits us if we don't *fear* God. To some, believing in Hell is a necessity, and to others it is just conceptualism. People will argue that it is impossible to have a Heaven without a Hell. In reality it is how we want to see the world and how we live in it that becomes the basis of our creation. That which manifests itself in a personal reality can be conditioned on a belief.

Hell and the Devil are crucial in creating an adversary of God in order to establish the mythology of "Good vs. Evil," sustaining a story that is read over and over. Historians will support with their findings that this belief lays the foundation for almost all mythologies and ancient religious practices. When those in power wish to control, they revert back to evil or Satan, just as parents revert to the "boogie man," to impose their will on their children — fear is used as a tool to control.

Hell, as it seems, is a greater drama of salvation from an impending event represented as a terrifying apocalypse. Hell became an attraction with "hellfire sermons" preached in large tents, which painted a gloomy picture of doom. Would you not agree that fear is a great tool to persuade people to do exactly what you want of them?

Do we live in fear or do we choose love in how we deal with our day-to-day experiences? It is for you, the individual, to choose to continue to suffer or experience bliss with every choice. This idea is something that I have to remind myself of constantly. Will I approach a new dilemma with fear or with a sense of bliss?

There is one thing I must mention about those who follow religious principles. Religion is a personal bond or sets of rules for life; it is obedience to a divine source, which to the devout follower offers *hope*. This is an important concept regardless of the validity of any dogma. The idea of *hope* enables some individuals to circumvent the ill experiences of life. Hope at times is a temporary panacea or Band-Aid for an unknown outcome. Hope soothes the heart and allows one to apply acceptance even if it is done blindly. Hope at times can effect a psychological and or emotional state that allows individuals to feel better about something they are not in control of.

From my perspective, one should not subscribe to a religious practice if it promotes separatism. We cannot believe that our religion is the "true religion," and all others practice a "false religion" and worship a false god. Religion can be positive if we accept its practice as a product of our culture, thereby expressing all the beauty that a given culture can offer. If we can respect the exquisiteness within all cultures we can maintain balance and agree that all are different paths for living and are representations of that group's perspective in life. There is nothing wrong with "believing" if we don't represent it as an *absolute* truth.

There are many people who profess to be religious, yet their actions stand against every basic concept of what their religion professes. They are religious when it serves them, and they are guilty of being immoral when it serves them. They feel justified by going to church on Sunday yet lying under oath in court on Monday after putting their hand on the Bible. These individuals are not connected to spirituality. They are simply customizing their beliefs in order to serve their personal agenda regardless of whom they hurt or how. This is an application of ego, and thus a separation from other people.

I have witnessed religious preachers offer sermons and salvation to the poor while collecting large sums of love offerings (money). In turn, these tithes allow the preacher to purchase luxury cars and live in upscale neighborhoods that are inaccessible to those they are preaching salvation to. "Megachurches" are "megasources" of income.

I have also witnessed soldiers during wartime go to Mass in the morning only to kill innocent people later in the day. It doesn't make sense to me. It is amazing what one can learn by simply observing human behavior and hypocritical belief more closely.

It seems that throughout history religious cultures perpetuate war in order to serve their own interest all the while dehumanizing other cultures. The war that I personally experienced in Vietnam had nothing to do with love; it in itself was an act of evil. As I mentioned earlier, statistically 80% of war casualties in Vietnam were considered "collateral damage." In other words, innocent women, children, and the elderly were killed as a function of war.

One might ask what all of this has to do with the difference between religion and spirituality. The difference lies in how spirituality is represented and manifested by the individual. Religion applies to a fundamental belief in a set of scriptures, considered to be holy, represented by a Holy Spirit that exists only through faith. This is how spirituality is defined through religious ideology. In contrast, the spirituality that has been given to me, by my spirit guide and through my life experiences, is a totally different concept.

Spirituality involves a heightened awareness by way of connection, communion, or communication with multidimensional entities that may represent, and are not limited to, the Godhead, Creators, spirit guides, angels, multidimensional human spirits, or extraterrestrial beings. Spirituality, as I define it, is void of religious properties that promote fear, damnation, or salvation. It is an awareness of human potential and is at the very essence of our struggle to disclose the mysteries of life.

The purpose of spirituality is to live by way of creativity, fulfillment, deeply rooted contentment, and knowing through awareness. It offers the understanding and practice to support a balanced life in mind, body, and spirit, void of ego and unnecessary struggle, promoting a life characterized by graceful love. This idea invites us to live in a way that both reflects and develops wisdom, love, joy, vitality, empowerment, peace, authenticity, passion, curiosity, appreciation, pleasure, trust, gratitude, and an unrelenting engagement in remembering who we really are — a spirit being. Furthermore, this philosophy is grounded in the knowledge that these qualities are characteristic of our true and fundamental nature. They are our inherent and undying birthright to evolve spiritually to unconditional love for ourselves, family, community, nature, and the human race.

Spirituality can be used to heal ourselves not only emotionally but also physically. Practicing *Balík* Meditation, or similar meditations, may guide one to awareness for a better life and overall wellness. In some cases the idea "Heal the mind, heal the body" is effective in overall wellness. At the very least, meditation is a foundation for acceptance during troubling periods in your life. I have witnessed how one's outlook in life can be altered by meditation. With constant practice you can learn to express positive thoughts within every aspect of your life.

Is religion a bad thing? I say "no" if one is also open to outside disciplines and is not a prisoner to dogma. This is necessary to adjust one's belief system for any potential controlling factors that are within religious tenets. This is not as common as I would like, but I do know of people who use their religion to fulfill their lives without any controlling factors or adverse effects. They are well-balanced individuals and are making religion work for them in a healthy manner. However, they are few.

In my experience, the closest way to "God" is a direct personal connection, and not through the minds of other men or women who create and preach dogma. I often look within a specific religion to see if it adheres to what I have experienced. In other words, if a religion says only their prophet and no other is capable of rising from the dead, then I know this is a false claim because I have had personal experiences with family members appearing to me after death in solid form. Skeptics will say I am hallucinating, and I will say their dogma is wrong... dead wrong. If a religion says that common people aren't capable of knowing the mysteries of life, I say they are again, dead wrong. One has to look at the weak arguments in a belief system. If there is one faulty argument, then it is safe to say there may be more weak areas in their belief or logic.

The next time you are in a discussion with a group of people try counting the number of times you or the other person uses the term "I believe" instead of facts to support each person's argument. Many people will not question their belief; they are stuck to it because they are tenacious and will commit fearful acts to defend it.

I do not "believe" in anything. I subscribe to *knowing.* If I do not know something for sure, such as having an actual experience, then I do not support it with "I believe." If I have an intuitive feeing about something due to my research, then I use the term "I feel." By using the term "I feel," I am not guilty of promoting an idea as a certainty or as an absolute. It is open to change with newfound knowledge or experiences — believing creates ignorance, and ignorance breeds fear.

With this in mind, I *feel* that most religions and ideologies are supported with belief systems and not facts. Belief systems, in some instances, are built upon logical fallacies and falsehoods that in turn engender fear in order to gain support from people who are directed to create ill-fated experiences for the masses, such as wars and immoral atrocities — let us not forget the Spanish Inquisition of 1478.

At times a belief is potentially dangerous to the human experience. An example of this danger is war that is brought about by a difference of belief. At the time of this writing there are faithful Muslims and faithful Christians who are killing one another and committing immoral acts. Is that what Jesus really wished for us, to kill others who don't believe as we do? I am sure this can be argued. However, according to the Bible, Jesus was most indignant when he was in a religious temple. Perhaps he witnessed men creating their own self-serving beliefs instead of listening to the message. If Jesus were to come back today I *feel* he would shout out, "No! That is not what I meant!" Perhaps Jesus supported spirituality, not religion, since he was feared by the religious leaders of the current popular religion at the time — he was crucified.

In *A New Earth* (New York: Plume, 2005), Eckhart Tolle, writes:

> Many people are already aware of the difference between spirituality and religion. They realize that having a belief system — a set of thoughts that you regard as the absolute truth — does not make you spiritual no matter what the nature of those beliefs is. In fact, the more you make your thoughts (beliefs) into your identity, the more cut off you are from the spiritual dimension within yourself. (p. 17)

One can see that Eckhart Tolle's statement sheds light on the errors within belief systems. Therefore, I am not alone in challenging belief systems. However, my observation is that a significant percentage of people are moving toward concepts of spirituality outside of those presented by religions. They know it is OK to know

God in a different way than what has been tenaciously presented to them from generation to generation.

We must ask ourselves if the religion we are practicing represents unconditional love in every idea and action pertaining to politics, economics, and morality. Is the religion that I have faith in guilty of preaching ideas that have parameters? Does it allow the individual to think critically, or does the religion do the thinking for me?

There is nothing more detrimental to an individual's growth than a changeless state. We must be open to how we look at our world and to our way of thinking and make an effort to change when we need to. We must be aware of and scrutinize the beliefs that we are creating because they may not be a representation of love or truth. Even what I have written here can easily change with further experiences. I am not locked into an ideology — truth is my goal. It does take energy to seek truth, but the truth is worth time and energy as it benefits one and all.

Mark Twain once said, "Man is the only animal that loves his neighbor as himself and cuts his throat if his religion isn't straight." And Blaise Pascal said, "Men never do evil so completely and so cheerfully as when they do it from religious convictions." We have witnessed historically how tenacious, inflexible religious ideologies, even when they preach love, lead their adherents to commit evil acts to impose their will upon fellow human beings. Discovering love based on truth will serve all of humanity to ensure human dignity — thus enacting God's love as we love and accept one another.

TWELVE

Angels, Ghosts, and Spirits

"I don't believe that ghosts are 'spirits of the dead' because I don't believe in death.
In the multi-universe, once you're possible, you exist. And once you exist, you exist
forever one way or another. Besides, death is the absence of life, and the ghosts I've
met are very much alive. What we call ghosts are lifeforms just as you and I are."

PAUL F. ENO, *FOOTSTEPS IN THE ATTIC*

Angels, ghost, and spirits… are they real? If so, where do they come from? If not, why are so many people having experiences with this type of phenomenon? These are questions that a large percentage of the population asks. More often than not, these types of experiences are commonly referred to as "figments of the imagination" of creative minds, not to mention a popular topic for Hollywood screenwriters to entertain the public with digital images meant to scare us.

Many individuals admit they have some level of fascination with the supernatural and claims of ghost encounters that are mentioned in the media. These people are looking to be entertained with no intention of giving serious thought to the possibility of life after death. On the other hand, a few admit to having paranormal experiences with spirits and seek answers. They desire information — guidance toward the truth — the ultimate truth.

I will share my experiences with my readers, but also explain and give reasons why I and many others possess the gift of discernment and Induced Knowledge. I feel we were given this gift in order to help others to decipher the meanings and origins of their paranormal experiences.

It was the summer of 1956 when I had my first spiritual encounter at the innocent age of five. Not able to reason with the experience at such a young age, I never thought how that encounter would connect me to the spirit world.

My experience came full circle thirty-one years later when my father appeared to me in physical form a few months after his death in 1987. My life changed with that experience, and a chain of events caused me to further investigate the paranormal.

I tried to make sense of how it was possible for my father to reappear after death, not in a translucent or ghostly form, but in human flesh, breathing, and talking. He was brought back to life as if manifested from one dimension to another.

If Jesus could rise from the dead and appear to his apostles two thousand years ago, then why can't such miracles occur in our lifetime? Miracles have occurred in my life, not once, but many times.

Since most "believe" that communication from the Godhead or spirit world was possible before and during the time of Jesus, then isn't it possible that communication is happening to us today? Open yourself to the idea that the great mystery of life is no mystery at all. All one needs to learn is to open and center the mind, body, and spirit. This will give you the ability to listen when "God" or your spirit guides communicate with you with silent internal words, thoughts, feelings, and most of all experiences.

The experience I had at the age of five was simple and complex at the same time. I woke up in the middle of the night to a man and a woman standing at the entrance to my brother's bedroom. I had a perfect view of his doorway from the position of my bed. I could see the couples' backs as they stood gazing for a few minutes into his room. I thought it was my aunt and uncle, or friends of my parents, so I turned around and tried to fall back asleep.

A few moments later I had a feeling that someone was staring at me. When I turned to look, the couple was standing at my door, and now were gazing at me yet not saying a word or making any movement. I did not recognize either of these people. Even though I could see the shape of their faces, they were not identifiable.

The man was wearing a dark suit, and the woman was wearing a black top and a black pleated skirt with large, orange polka dots. They looked as if they were dressed up to go out for the evening. I didn't know them, so I ducked under the covers in an attempt to hide from strangers who were staring at me for a long period of time! I covered my head until I fell asleep.

The next morning, I asked my mother while she was cooking breakfast who the people were in our house last night. My mother stated there was no one else in our house, and I was just imagining it or having a dream. It seemed to be a logical explanation for a child to accept. I sat down to have my breakfast. Five minutes later, my brother walked into the kitchen and asked my mother the same questions.

My brother described the same couple, including what they were wearing, and it matched everything that I had seen. He said they first were looking into his room and then turned to look into my room. I jumped up out of my chair immediately and told my mother, "You see! I knew I wasn't dreaming!" I was excited because I had a witness and thought that two people couldn't be wrong!

My mother's answer was, "You both were imagining the same thing." Since we were children, we accepted her explanation.

Perhaps my mother knew there were spirits in the house but did not want to scare us. Or, she truly didn't know of anyone other than our family in our home; therefore, we were guilty of active imaginations.

Our society is not short of skeptics when it comes to spirits, ghosts, and other paranormal phenomena. Skeptics make the effort to debunk psychic ability and other paranormal topics using scientific reasoning. There are individuals who "claim" to be legitimate psychics who use different techniques such as the ideomotor effect, facilitated communication, hypnotic suggestions, and cold readings in order to convince their audiences they have spiritual powers, when in fact they don't. However, there are legitimate psychics who have published their experiences — void of all illusion. It is for you to decipher.

How do you interpret your personal experiences when it comes to the supernatural? If you have had an experience, do you believe it was real? Most people don't trust their experiences because of their fear of the unknown. They brush them off, store the memories in their subconscious, and mentally disassociate themselves from the encounters.

Those who discount the idea of paranormal activity are bound by their sense of logic and need for scientific empiricism to explain what reality is. Perhaps scientists will never experience it for themselves. If they do, will they label it with a scientific term that falls under the category of a mental or physiological dysfunction? This is convenient for the skeptic because a scientific explanation allows us to live within a man-made design without any supernatural consideration.

When we experience the feeling of being in the same place before, we simply call it *déjà vu*. We merely give it a fancy name and forget about the dynamics of the experience. When we get a premonition, we label it as a "gut feeling" not needing to understand it further. It's easier to approach it this way. Many find it safer to be scientific than spiritual because science is more logical and widely accepted.

Those who *believe* that any representation of a ghost/spirit is Satan are closed to anything outside of their religious faith. Therefore most of these individuals will evolve within their own belief system — if it isn't of God, it is of Satan.

It is your free will that will guide you to your personal reality, wrong or right. Let those who choose to be controlled continue in their belief, and let those who prefer to know the truth come to a higher awareness.

Angels

Angels may come in various forms; however, many agree that most are either human spirits or angelic nonhuman entities. I have mentioned before that I feel benevolent extraterrestrials may have also been mistaken or identified as angels by ancient cultures.

One form of angel is known as the "Earth Angel," a human who is reincarnated not only to evolve to an even higher level, but also to help others in special ways. They constantly cross paths with people so they may affect them with guidance and love.

A spiritual gift is usually associated with the Earth Angel so they may be effective in their work on Earth. Earth Angels usually don't consciously know they are angels; they aren't supposed to know unless they figure it out on their own or receive Induced Knowledge. An example of an Earth Angel would be Mother Teresa, and a common example would be a spiritual healer or perhaps an Earth guide (a person who guides others toward spirit consciousness).

Angels (Latin: *angelus*; Greek: *aggelos*;) are either divine or human messengers. The Bible describes angels as spiritual beings that connect God to mankind. Angels instruct, guide, and foretell future events.

The Bible implies that each person has his or her own "guardian angel." Could they be classified as spirit guides? Perhaps it is only a matter of semantics. Nonetheless, a guardian angel is a multidimensional being, which means many religions subscribe to the supernatural. If you study various religions you will find passages describing angels and their purpose in serving humankind.

Archetypes of angels have been developed according to various cultures and belief systems, but we can all agree they are very similar in their depiction and function. I don't know if they are human spirits, extraterrestrial entities, or other types of manifested energy. What I do know is what I have experienced with my personal spirit guide — to know my truth is to experience it for yourself as I have.

Laura Lee, the psychic medium and very dear friend with whom I worked on *X-Ops*, describes on her website *messagesoflove.com* what an angel medium is. She states:

> An angel is a messenger or harbinger. A medium is an individual held to be a channel of communication between earthly and spirit worlds. This means they have the ability to consciously receive inspiring messages, often revealing past, present and future, from dearly departed, including guides and guardian angels. The messages can be received through clairvoyance (inner sight), claircognizance (knowing), clairsentience (feeling), and or through clairaudience (inner hearing).

Ghosts

The belief in ghosts dates back to preliterate cultures. Ghosts are typically described as translucent or hazy images. They may take the form of a dark silhouette or a blur. They may be seen at times to be floating in the air. Some believe the spirit world is in another dimension that is approximately three feet above our ground level. Physical laws are different in that dimension they will say; therefore our perspective will be different.

Ghosts are usually lost souls trapped in between this dimension and the dimension of the spirit world. Unlike spirits, ghost are unable to move back and forth between dimensions at will — they do not have the knowledge to go "into the light" on their own. They will need guidance from other spirits or from humans in this dimension. Some ghosts do not believe they are dead and will continue to live their usual lives in our earthly dominion. They can see us in the physical realm, but most of the time we cannot see them unless we are sensitive to their frequency, have psychic abilities, or they choose to be seen.

Some ghosts can be frustrated and will act out in order to get our attention. They will try to communicate by any means necessary and will resort to mischief as they discover newfound talents such as moving objects, affecting electronics at will, or walking through walls. There are times when ghosts will follow a person or family from one residence to another and will continue, as some put it, to "haunt" them. I would estimate that over half of the homes that I have lived in have had a spirit or ghost present. If you encounter a presence in your home, there is no need to be alarmed. You may be scared, but the presence will not hurt you. However, if you are bothered and afraid, you can use techniques to rid the presence from your home.

To do this, you will need to "smoke" the home with sage or incense, salt the doorways and windows, burn a white candle, and pray for the ghosts. Remember that the use of these tools is a means to give your thoughts direction. The value of these rituals is found in the intention and thought, not in the tool. Surround your home in prayer within the "White Light of Divinity" and ask all negative entities to leave in the name of the Lord Father, the Creator, the Holiest of Spirits, and/or Jesus Christ. In your prayer, tell the spirits or ghosts they are dead and not to be afraid of leaving. They must find the light and go to it. Make sure to express it in a firm and loving way especially when you want to claim your home.

Bless them and tell them their loved ones are waiting for them on the other side. Tell them they are no longer welcome in your home and they must leave so you and they may have peace.

Spirits

A spirit is an entity that previously was alive or not and is able to move from one dimension to the next at will. Spirits cannot be seen in the standard sense unless they want to be seen; one needs to either be gifted with the ability to see them or they will willingly appear into this dimension so they may be seen by whomever they choose. When they materialize it is usually for a reason and only to certain people.

The spirits that are with us constantly are spirit guides or guardian angels, and they are here to help us and inform us. When we get a message or knowledge from our inner voice it is considered communication from them. Sometimes, you know something is going to happen. You don't know how you know, but you do know that *something* will actually occur — then it does. Some people call it a "gut feeling," intuition, or even coincidence.

My advice is for you to practice developing this natural gift because we all have it. Anyone can develop it; one needs to be conscious of it first. It is one way our spirit guides communicate with us. Most of us don't listen to our silent voice; we *believe* it is useless internal dialogue.

The next time you get a "gut feeling" you should file this feeling in your memory. Try to remember how you were told (or how you told yourself) and what the mental and physical feeling was. If you can remember these things you can build on it, learn to receive it, and listen to it for guidance. It is for a reason that we experience this and the interpretation of the experiences can be a very powerful tool for life. Make sure you also give thanks by acknowledging that you understand. I usually say, "I hear you. Thank you." The spirit world likes confirmation. It is rewarding to your spirit guide.

I had a spirit in my studio, but I was not alarmed. My friend Lynette, who had no psychic ability, had seen it when she was visiting and told me the apparition she saw was an older gentleman. I experienced the spirit later on and thought it interesting the way it was getting my attention by knocking objects off the counter multiple times and turning the television off while I was watching a program.

I was fine with all that had happened until the spirit bothered a client during business hours. I had to smoke my studio and ask the spirit to leave because he grabbed my client's back, which scared him.

Perhaps the spirit thought it should scare the client by grabbing him or simply wanted the client to know it was there. It did the job. My client approached me and reported that someone had just grabbed him and asked me if something weird was going on in my studio. He freaked out when I said, "Yea, there's a spirit in here."

I can't emphasize how important *intention* is when it comes to having control. When one is in control, one has no fear — it really is that simple. It takes practice to feel that way and it is a lot safer when dealing with multidimensional beings — good and bad.

"Spirit manifestations" are spirits that appear in the physical form, as in a full-body apparition. They exist as if they are alive. They speak and breathe. They touch and are capable of being touched.

Imagine that you have just buried a family member. You were at the funeral where the body was interred. A month later, you are exiting the supermarket and loading your groceries into your car when this very same family member walks up to you and says "Hello." You are shocked then thrilled because this person is alive, or at least that is your first thought. You hug the person, who feels warm to the touch, and you are in a loving experience. The person tells you not to worry about him/her and that he/she loves you. After a short dialogue, which may or may not involve a profound message, the family member turns and walks away.

I guarantee that you will not *believe* what just happened to you. Well-meaning friends will offer many explanations: "You were sad about losing the person, and in your mind you wanted to see them because you probably miss them or have some guilt." This is not the truth. You know what you saw and felt, but you just don't know how to explain it. With time you question your experience. It is easier to fall prey to the reasoning that you were hallucinating. Unfortunately time goes by and you forget about it, and you may continue to wonder if it was real or not. Eventually you will doubt yourself and the experience — society's way of controlling you.

These types of experiences will complicate most people's lives. Most don't want to be known as a person who sees spirits or hears voices. They will think no one will believe them, except for someone like me. However, I would not *believe*, I have no need for belief; I would *feel* they had an actual experience because I *know* it is possible. They believe there will be no support from those around them, therefore, they would rather discount the truth of what they experienced. It's possible it will be buried in the subconscious forever.

Please understand that an experience like this is a gift of knowledge from the spirit world. You were given a *knowing* about the created mystery of life. The experience was designed for you to evolve to a higher consciousness. Do not blow it off and stay ignorant to the essence of the spirit world. Do not be one of those people who need a ton of bricks to hit them on the head in order to know what is real.

In other chapters you will read about my experience with spirits that have manifested into this dimension. I consider them gifts of love that were given to me for a reason. With these gifts I am reminded of who I am: a spirit first and a personality second.

At the center of most indigenous cultures is a spiritual practice. To be more accurate, they are belief systems that connect the spiritual world to the natural world.

When there is manipulation for personal power and its motivation is to instill fear, then one is tapping into the dark side of the belief system. Therefore, look at your belief system and conclude if any part of it supports the dark side, which includes war and greed. Does your group involve itself in promoting political agendas that support the concept of "Good vs. Evil" as a justification for war? If it does, then your group leaders may be directing its members toward the "dark side." This is masking a dark side that promotes evil deeds in the name of faith. It induces fear and is void of love.

Casting spells on others through incantations and rituals can only have an effect if the supposedly "cursed" person believes he/she is being altered by the spell. The mind is powerful and vulnerable to suggestion especially when one has a belief based on fear that an event or action will alter one's health, luck, or even one's life. It is my experience there is nothing that another human being can do to you with magic if you do not allow it. Therefore, our thoughts are powerful and we can control our environment with positive thinking and by focusing on love, which is supported by spirit guides and angels.

I was discussing with a Christian friend the possibilities of the existence of demons and Satan. I mentioned to her that in all the experiences I have had with spirits I have never encountered an evil one. Not that evil spirits don't exist; but, rather, I have never had an encounter with one.

I admitted I had a few spirits engage in mischievous pranks. However, their actions were merely attempts to get my attention, not to scare me. I told her about a little boy's spirit that lifted the blanket slightly off my bed so it could lie next to me because it didn't want to be alone. She freaked out upon hearing this. I explained to her it was something a live child would do out of fear or loneliness. If you view these actions with a sense of fear, then they can be spooky. Spirits have never harmed me in any way — so far. Perhaps I have been lucky.

My friend explained that she experienced something she described as a *demon*. When she woke up she saw a stranger sitting at the foot of her bed. She judged it as an evil presence that stared at her as she lay frozen with fear. She described the demon as an older man, and she could barely make out his face or what he was wearing. She was so afraid, she closed her eyes and prayed in the name of Jesus, and the stranger disappeared once she reopened her eyes.

I asked her, "Was the man grotesque-looking in any way?"

She answered, "No."

I asked, "Did he have fangs or horns?" Her answer again was no. "Did he touch you or hurt you in any way?" Still the answer was no. Then I asked her, "Did he look at you in a mean or awful way?"

She responded, "He was smiling at me."

I responded with, "So after our analysis, you are telling me you woke up and a man was sitting at the edge of your bed. He didn't touch you or hurt you and all he was doing was smiling at you in a loving manner?" My friend confirmed this was true. I continued, "Did you ever consider this person could have been your guardian angel or your spirit guide? You do believe in angels don't you?"

"Yes," she said.

I continued with, "What if you were given an experience of the highest manner, a realization that there are spirits and they are here to help and protect you? What if this was a family member who you don't know? What if this spirit was smiling at you to convey love and when he saw you were afraid he chose to leave?"

She stated, "I never thought about it that way."

My friend was conditioned to live in fear as many are when they adhere to a belief system that depicts all things unknown as evil. Some beliefs habitually degrade experiences when it comes to concepts outside of their ideology, especially if it involves spirits or the spirit world. In reality, when something is foreign to us, we sometimes develop a sense of fear of the unknown and we act accordingly.

My friend described her experience as one of fear from the onset of her vision. And perhaps she subconsciously categorized this spirit as a demon rather than a guardian angel or a loving spirit caught in transition. With further knowledge she will learn to adjust.

I am not discounting that fear is a normal reaction when one experiences this type of phenomenon. For most people, this form of experience, especially when new, is very scary. But it relates to the fear of the unknown, and triggers our *fight or flight* reaction. It is easier to label the unknown as evil when fear is a byproduct of the experience.

We need to accept the fact that we are sharing this world with angels, spirits, and ghosts in the past, present, and future, in this dimension and in all other dimensions. Their presence exists for a purpose. Perhaps with further research and documentation we will gain knowledge and accept that the spirit world is here to serve us and is truly alive and well.

Innocent Spirits

"It is wonderful that five thousand years have now elapsed since the creation of the
world, and still it is undecided whether or not there has ever been an instance of the spirit
of any person appearing after death. All argument is against it; but all belief is for it."

SAMUEL JOHNSON

Some spirits are unaware they have died, and continue to live as if they were still
in this physical dimension. These spirits at times are frustrated because they are
trapped between two worlds and tend to be mischievous in their encounters with
living humans. I must reiterate that I have never had a negative experience with
an evil or demonic form of spirit in any of my paranormal encounters. I have even
asked my spirit guide if it is necessary for me to have an encounter with a negative
entity to validate the existence of negative beings so I may be brought closer to the
whole truth.

Perhaps the reason I have not had negative experiences is because I do not adhere
to notions of evil and have been given the gift of Induced Knowledge, which is
grounded in the idea that love overpowers evil. Those who do believe in evil spirits
do so because the basis of their experience is fear, the opposite of love. You may
ask me, "So, Richard, are you confirming that evil demons and spirits do exist?" My
answer is, it depends on whether or not you are living in fear. In my case, I do not
give energy to evil.

There are spirits that are exempt from the full process of their transition. Meaning,
a person may pass away but does not make his or her journey to the other world.
This can be investigated by events involving innocent children who have died and
are trapped in between the world of the living and the world of the spirit. These
young spirits may scare people who are unaware that these spirits are children who

do not intend to cause fear or to even haunt people; they are merely trying to find love or comfort — they are innocent. This idea is embodied in an experience that happened to my former girlfriend and her sister while sharing an apartment in Corona, California, in 1994.

I would visit my girlfriend and her sister every weekend at their residence and on one occasion, when I entered the apartment, I smelled cigarette smoke. I asked the women if someone had been smoking, and they both said "no." I then asked them to stand by the hall entrance, and they both confirmed the existence of the odor.

A few hours later my girlfriend entered the rest room immediately after I exited. When she came out, she complained that I had been smoking a cigarette in the restroom. Denying it, I reentered the restroom to find that it did smell like someone was smoking and at the same time, I received Induced Knowledge that a spirit was present in the apartment.

I investigated further to see if cigarette smoke was possibly coming through the ventilation system of our neighbors below and found no occupants in the apartment. Although I knew what was happening, the women decided it was "nothing," and at the end of the day we went to sleep without any further discussion.

The next morning, my girlfriend's sister reported she felt someone lying on top of her during the night. She explained that she woke up and felt a person cuddling up to her side and on top of her. She was frightened, then tried to ignore it, and eventually fell back asleep.

The following weekend, my girlfriend's sister again reported not only did she feel someone on top of her, but felt someone kissing her on her cheeks. This of course frightened both women so I directed the sister to tell the spirit to leave her alone if it came back again.

On my third weekend visit to Corona, I woke up during the night to a distinctive aroma of barbecued chicken. I loved eating this type of chicken and had my girlfriend prepare it for me often.

I initially thought someone in the downstairs apartment was cooking but the apartment below us was vacant. Thinking the women had left the oven on, I got out of bed to check the kitchen. I clearly saw that the oven was off and there was nothing inside. At this moment, my spirit guide communicated to me that the guest spirit was in our bedroom and used the enticing aroma of chicken to lure me out of the room so it could climb into the bed with my girlfriend.

I quickly reentered the bedroom and focused as I stood near the entrance of the darkened room. I felt an energy presence of someone else standing and staring at me. After a few moments I crawled into bed and pretended to fall asleep to see what the spirit was planning to do.

Fifteen minutes passed. Then the corner of the blanket on my right side was lifted, and I felt pressure on the bed as if someone was getting under the covers next to me. I sat up and slammed the covers down with my right arm — hitting my clenched fist onto the bed. I must admit the experience was a little eerie, and I had to remind myself that these spirits are not evil, just a little mischievous.

I again pretended to be asleep for another few minutes when I felt someone crawl into the bed at my feet. Someone grazed my left leg, and I saw a body form under the blankets. I sat up to see that my girlfriend's legs were not near mine, and knew once again the spirit was trying to reenter the bed with us.

I sat up quickly and for the second time slammed down my arm onto the covers to discourage the uninvited visitor. This time I warned the spirit in a firm voice that I knew what it was attempting to do, and I would not allow it. I told it to leave and asked it not to bother us for the rest of the night. For the third time, I pretended to fall asleep but this time there was no further interruption from the spirit.

The following morning my girlfriend's sister came into our bedroom to report the spirit visited her again. She shared with us how the spirit was lying on her while trying to kiss her on the cheeks. When she told it to go away, as I instructed her to do, she heard it speak. The spirit said it would not bother her but it would be under her bed. The sister's curiosity got the best of her, so she slowly peeked under the bed skirt. To her surprise she found a little boy around the age of seven or eight lying in a fetal position under her bed.

My girlfriend was scared and demanded I do whatever it would take to get rid of the child spirit. I tried to reason with her that the spirit was an innocent child and did not want to harm or scare anyone. All he wanted was to be loved and comforted, and was probably scared and did not know where he was.

Knowing the experience was frightening to the women, I smoked and blessed the apartment and guided the spirit to the white light with loving words and affection. I informed him that he had died and his mother was waiting for him on the other side. All he had to do was follow my directions as I guided him to the white light.

Who knows how long this child had been wandering between two worlds with no clue as to where or what was happening to him. We must remember that spirits were human once, and they deserve the respect and love we should give one another here in this physical world. If we learn to understand the process of death — in reality a transitioning — and communicate love we can help these lost souls to the spirit world with direction and guidance.

We need to *try* to be unafraid of spirits. When we realize spirits may at times be our spirit guides or guardian angels, we will understand we are the ones who benefit from their existence. They are here to give us guidance and information so we may evolve spiritually in this world. We have to accept it is part of our human existence to acknowledge the other world where spirits reside — as indigenous people have for centuries.

Perhaps you have heard one of your family member's children talking about an imaginary friend. Your first reaction is the child has a vivid imagination. In reality, the imaginary friend is a spirit guide visiting the child to play with or care for the child. Sometimes it is a deceased family member playing the role of spirit guide or guardian angel. I have recorded many of these types of experiences.

My mother relayed such a story to me. She and my sister, Dianna, were driving with Dianna's grandson, Joshua, who was four years old at the time. He was sitting in a car seat in the back when my mother heard Joshua talking to someone then laughing. My mother asked Joshua whom he was talking to. He said, "My friend." My sister told my mother that Joshua had an imaginary friend who played with him often. My mother, Joshua's great-grandmother, asked Joshua what his friend's name was. Joshua answered, "Gilbert." He paused, looked to his left, and then corrected himself, "He says his name is Grandpa Gilbert." To my mom's amazement Joshua was identifying my father, Joshua's great-grandfather. Both were thinking it was a coincidence that his friend's name was Gilbert.

After my mother told this story to me, she asked me, "Could it be possible that your father is Joshua's imaginary friend?" I explained to her that children are very susceptible to seeing spirits up until the age of four or five. They are still sensitive to spirits and are even able to communicate with spirits. After four or five years old, their keen spiritual sense wears off.

I took out a large family photo that pictured my father, mother, siblings, and myself, and I showed it to Joshua. I asked him who some of these people were, and as I pointed to each, he named every one of them. I pointed to my father and asked him if he knew who he was, and Joshua paused for a moment then said, "That's my friend, Gilbert. But sometimes he calls himself Grandpa Gilbert." What makes this very interesting is Joshua had never met his great-grandfather or had even seen a picture of him, and we never referred to him as "Gilbert."

Joshua was born seven years after my father passed away. I feel my father is Joshua's spirit guide and is very active spiritually with my family even to this day at my mother's home where Joshua lives. My family has love for one another, and my father has always been at the base of that love even after his transition.

There is no doubt my father is still in my mother's home. I have felt his presence on occasion, and during a family gathering he showed me he was there. My mother has an antique glass cabinet in her living room. It can be seen if one is sitting in the large family room near the entrance area. As I was sitting at a table and conversing with family members I turned to my right and saw the door of the cabinet open on its own. I thought it odd so I walked over to it and tried to make sense of what I witnessed. I checked for a strong draft. I closed it and opened it a few times to see if it could easily be opened. There was no wind, and once the door is shut it needs some force to open it.

Standing in front of the cabinet I was given a mental message that my father was opening the cabinet door to let me know he was there. Standing alone, and focused on what I was about to say, I acknowledged my father, then asked him to open the door again — it opened. There was one person who I felt needed to experience this.

I called my cousin Kenny to come over. His father passed away earlier that year. I wanted him to experience this in order to confirm what I had shared with him about life after death when his father passed. I expressed to him our spirit lives on, and death is not a reality — I offered him an experience as proof of what I know to be true.

With Kenny standing next to me, I asked him to observe what I was about to do. I told him my father was opening the door in order to communicate that he was here. I asked Kenny to open the cabinet door so he could feel the amount of effort it took to open it. After he opened and closed it a few times, I told him to pay attention. I asked my father to open it, and as soon as I asked, the door opened wide. Kenny stood there with a big grin on his face. Although he was perplexed by what he witnessed, he didn't challenge what he experienced.

It is my personal feeling most spirits represent a form of innocence, and they allow us to see them for a reason. We are at times conditioned to *believe* they are here to scare us or harm us, and Hollywood plays a big role in exploiting this fear. Many books and movies capitalize on the spooky and scary version of spirits and the supernatural, so no wonder we are always afraid as a society.

What we don't understand, we choose to fear. Once we do understand, we will learn to love the essence of life and our transition, and how both will serve us. Learning the value of spirit guides and to use the information and teachings we receive from them will ultimately make life more pleasant with spiritual love for not only the innocent spirits, but for all who have departed.

FOURTEEN

Sleep Paralysis

"When, doomed to death I shall have expired, I will attend you as
a nocturnal fury; and, a ghost, I will attack your faces with my hooked
talons (for such is the power of those divinities, the Manes) and brooding
upon your restless breasts, I will deprive you of repose by terror."

HORACE, *5TH EPODE*

Those of us who have experienced sleep paralysis will report that it is not only odd, but frightening. This condition can happen just before falling asleep or right before awakening. The one having the experience is paralyzed and unable to speak or scream. What is eerie about this phenomenon is the feeling of a presence, usually described as evil, in the room, with the purpose of observing you. This idea, along with being paralyzed, can cause one to panic.

When a person has an auditory, visual, or emotional experience during the paralysis it is recognized by researchers as either hallucinatory or delusional. I will argue not all experiences fall into either of those categories.

A famous painting by Henry Fuseli (1741–1825) depicts a woman reclining on a bed with a grotesque demon or incubus positioned on top of her with the malevolent intention of stealing her soul. The experience of feeling pressure on the chest while sleeping on one's back is historically referred to as "The Old Hag Attack."

In order to explain this phenomenon, I will present two perspectives, my own paranormal theory and a scientific theory that is void of spiritual or multidimensional concepts within its examination and conclusion. Although there are many studies on sleep paralysis available on the Internet, few researchers allow the public to submit experiences of their own to help gather data.

For a 1999 study of sleep paralysis, Allan J. Cheyne and associates from the University of Waterloo in Canada gathered data and published a journal for those interested in detailed scientific information on the subject. They developed a website that allows individuals to submit their experiences pertaining to this phenomenon. His study offers a scientific perspective relating to variations and similarities of events during sleep paralysis. From these surveys he collected data to show commonalities among a large group of respondents.

A finding from researchers shows there are higher incidences of sleep paralysis when one sleeps in the supine position (on one's back). Furthermore, according to scientific studies, the events of sleep paralysis, such as hallucinations, are results of disturbed REM (Rapid Eye Movement) sleep caused by life stressors or sleep deprivation.

There is ample research published about REM sleep, the stage of sleep in which you are dreaming, which states that all muscle activity is prevented from acting out one's dreams. This form of muscle paralysis is called atonia, which plays an important role in passing between the stages of sleep and wakefulness. When atonia fails, the disorder is referred to as REM Sleep Behavior Disorder (RBD). In the case of RBD, one is able to sleepwalk or move erratically during the sleep state. Therefore, one theory for sleep paralysis is when an individual wakes up or is about to sleep, atonia is malfunctioning by not allowing freedom of muscle movement, keeping the person in a state of paralysis.

In the surveys collected by Professor Cheyne, there are people who claim the ability to fly around the room and undergo other forms of phenomena such as out-of-body experiences. It is no wonder scientists, especially psychologists, would label these events as hallucinations. Some scientists even go so far as to propose the condition of sleep paralysis is responsible for claims of encounters with spirits and extraterrestrials such as alien abductions. I disagree with these findings simply because of my own experience with these types of entities. Simply said, I *know* they exist and researchers don't.

How can one argue with science when *your* reality falls into their convenient category of auditory or tactile hallucinations? Even more confusing would be scientists who have actually had paranormal experiences of their own but could not offer scientific proof. That would be an intricate and difficult problem — a real conundrum for sure. With all their efforts, I would imagine their colleagues would find them out of touch with reality and most likely shun them as incapable scientists with delusional views. Therefore, many scientists conclude it is better not to mention ideas of the paranormal within the scientific community if they want to be taken seriously. This is a problem I have with science. How can one break the barriers if one is in fear of being ridiculed or stigmatized?

My education is in psychology, but my life experiences are in the paranormal. I cannot disregard either view because I can reason from both perspectives. A growing number of people are becoming more open to ideas that were previously labeled as skewed. I am more interested in bringing forth a truth for these people, not scientists — who have already reached their own conclusions. It has been said that by the time science reaches the summit of truth in terms of the paranormal and mysticism, the mystic will already be waiting and asking, "What took you so long?"

How is it possible to have such a vivid experience, in an awakened state, with the only clear and logical account of your experience interpreted as, "You were in a state of hallucination"? When scientists conclude that alien abductions are related to sleep paralysis, they are actually making a claim that extraterrestrials do not exist. Therein lies the problem when one event can be submitted and correlated to another event that is not an acceptable reality. "You were hallucinating," is considered a rational societal explanation.

In cases of grotesque demons, I feel our subconscious mind-thought is *capable* of manifesting a demonic creature to fulfill our need to justify Satan's existence. We create this presence based on our limited information about entities from other dimensions. We envision what was taught to us and what our culture accepts through mythology. Therefore, when we experience something out of our conscious mind we adhere to these preformulated archetypes. Then again, who am I to say a person didn't *actually* experience a typical demonic archetype? One theory is that a negative multidimensional being is able to present itself according to what it reads within our subconscious mind, gaining energy from our fears. They can represent a demon if that is your fear.

My personal hypnopompic (when awakened) experience with sleep paralysis occurred in the year 2000 when I was living in Los Angeles, California. My mind was conscious of my surroundings but my body was paralyzed. My natural response was to become fearful, and I immediately tried to break loose from the paralysis. I felt the presence of another being in the room as others have reported, but because of my previous experiences with spirits I did not find the presence to be evil.

Although this phenomenon was new to me, I was compelled to stay in control in order to learn about this experience.

I have to admit that sleep paralysis is one of the strangest physical and psychological experiences I have ever had. It was the thought and feeling that someone or something was observing me that was unsettling, especially because I was in a state of helplessness. Rather than panic, I let the natural reaction of fear subside. I immediately calmed myself and decided to not fight what I was going through. I simply became the observer so I could make a mental record of what was happening. After the first few seconds I took mental notes of everything that I was feeling as if in a controlled clinical study.

Instead of expecting something demonic or evil I considered the possibility that I may have tuned into another frequency along with a multidimensional entity or spirit who was sharing time and space with me. As the seconds passed, the paralysis subsided, and I quickly documented what I was feeling during the brief ten-second period. As soon as I came out of the sleep paralysis I had Induced Knowledge that I was in between this dimension and the spirit world, as if affected by a different energy source. This supports why I felt the presence of another person or entity; I was sharing a space-time continuum (where space represents three dimensions, time is the fourth dimension, and the spirit world is the fifth), and was being observed by one or more entities. I theorized that sleep paralysis is a product of our own spirit finding itself positioned between two dimensions. There are times when our spirit enters the spiritual dimension where our thoughts affect our dreams. While we are in that dimensional state, our thoughts create dream scenarios.

Many scientists conduct their studies without considering the possibility of supernatural forces, extraterrestrial entities, or the existence of a spiritual dimension. Instead they focus and direct their studies toward the physiological or psychological aspects and may be missing potentialities of other types of phenomena. They will attribute symptoms of sleep paralysis to the effects of narcolepsy or other sleep disorders. Medication is another contributor according to some researchers.

It is a fact that the parameter of science limits paranormal research. However, there are a few scientists who are making strong efforts to use the scientific method to explore the paranormal, regardless of the threat of being stigmatized by peers. They are going beyond conventional research methods by developing new approaches either directly or indirectly to studying the paranormal. They are challenging the current acceptable idea that a large subpopulation is suffering from hallucinations when it comes to paranormal experiences.

It is common to label or categorize experiences as "hallucinations" and "delusions" if such characteristics are within the DSM-IV-TR, which is a product of psychology and scientific data.

Researchers will describe their findings using intellectual reasoning supported by the scientific method, which will satisfy their colleagues. In turn, findings are published in scientific journals and the researcher will eventually move on to the next area of study. The terms "possibly" or "maybe" are used to sustain their findings based on scientific statistical data. If one cannot contain it or observe it through systematic empirical (scientific) observation, it will be inconclusive and invalid.

Knowing this, I was still compelled to communicate via email with Professor Cheyne during his study on sleep paralysis. I explained to him that it is possible the demons experienced by many people in his studies were a byproduct of fear and preconceptions about what their religions teach. However, we must not underestimate the reality of other forms of dimensional beings such as spirit or alien entities that are capable of entering our dimension.

My wish is that I could have directed Professor Cheyne to a video I saw of a person having an experience of sleep paralysis. In this video, immediately afterward a lamp moves on its own as it knocks down a picture frame from a nightstand. How would one explain that? The person was previously having paranormal experiences in his bedroom, and wanted to capture it on film as proof.

Cheyne was open to hearing my theory on the phenomenon of sleep paralysis but I realized he could not give it much consideration. Although he did and continues to do an excellent job with his research and arrived at an interesting conclusion, I feel an important aspect was omitted.

Perhaps in the near future, science will be more willing to step out of the box when dealing with matters of the paranormal. However, public demand will need to prompt this type of investigation. My theory, based on personal experience and not capable of being measured scientifically, rests outside of the rules of science, and therefore, is of no use or value to researchers — which is fair, for now.

Most scientists have concluded that dreams are merely processed information. Moreover, while in sleep mode dreams make sense of an array of mental data collected during our daily lives.

Is it possible that ideas or visions stored in our subconscious mind will manifest themselves in our dreams? If we haven't programmed it in our mind through daily experiences, is it possible during sleep we have created them with our thoughts? What is the reasoning behind a dream that represents a specific meaning? Are nightmares affected by the subconscious mind and of our own creation, telling us something is wrong using symbolism? These are reasonable queries I present to question what is considered acceptable to scientists who study dreams and their meanings. At this time I feel our science is limited by the technology used to gather data in studying not only dreams but also the paranormal.

We can fly and perform very strange events in our dreams, and when these events are analyzed it is possible to understand what they mean and why they are formulated into dreams. For instance, I was riding a horse in a recurring dream, and the saddle kept slipping off the rear end of the horse. I was dangling in the wind behind the horse with the saddle underneath my body. I tried to pull myself up by yanking on the reins, but to no avail. I eventually fell off of the horse. I analyzed this dream and concluded that my subconscious mind was telling me I was not in control at that particular time in my life. My dream was not a case of my spirit entering another dimension — it was about having control — my subconscious mind was creating it to present a valid life issue.

As a spiritual counselor I have had clients report events I would categorize as sleep paralysis. Clients would describe the feeling of an evil presence in close proximity, as if someone was in the room watching them. Others would report they saw spirits standing at the foot or at the side of their bed. Most admitted they would usually feel pressure on their chest, claiming that Satan or a demon was on top of them communicating with them telepathically. One would think they were simply experiencing a traumatic nightmare. However, my findings present similarities in the experiences reported by people from different cultures and ages.

Although reports have been similar in nature, my findings suggest there are differences between entities that have been experienced during sleep paralysis. We know that the effects of sleep paralysis feel real to the sufferer, but we don't know why. Researchers aren't certain why people have frightening hallucinations, but they feel it is due to anxiety. Various treatments used include melatonin, a natural hormone, and antidepressants such as Zoloft or Prozac. These treatment options aren't presented as totally successful.

When awakened from a paralyzed state an individual may feel out of control and will react with a *fight or flight* response, which is an innate primordial survival tactic. In this case the person is paralyzed and experiencing an intense fear. The presence of someone in the room is extremely disconcerting especially if one considers it evil. One of my clients described a demonic-looking spirit with horns of a goat holding his arms, pinning him down, and staring with evil intent. Others report being choked either by something they can't see or by a demon-like creature. Of thirty people interviewed, 90% claim to have been awake and not dreaming when they experienced a demon or spirit, 80% state they had an experience seeing an entity immediately after waking up, 60% report having more than one such experience, and 40% suggest the room or home in which they had the experience they were reporting had already been the setting for some previous form of paranormal activity.

Our thoughts are very powerful, and it is possible that we can create an unsettling scenario if we tap into fear. Whenever we encounter a spirit in our home, we tend to define the spirit as being evil or categorize the experience as a haunting. Do we not get chills up and down our spine when we experience something we do not understand? Would you agree the unknown has its potential danger? Manuel Mora, a colleague of mine, defines fear as "uncontrollable excitement."

When one is having a vision of an entity, there is a potentiality to create or represent it as a demon archetype. When in a state of fear we are capable of creating demon images of what we have seen in books and movies. On the flip side of the coin, I feel that demons, or more precisely, negative entities, are a reality although not in the same capacity as we have been led to believe. We can't totally discount what people are reporting, we can only investigate their claims.

I realize my writings sometimes suggest I don't accept the demon theory while at other times asserts they do exist. This contradiction is due to a differentiation between what societies accept as demon archetypes and my experiences. The demons that I accept as a reality are bidimensional entities that are either negative extra-terrestrial or terrestrial beings, not Biblically associated demons that are followers of the fallen angel, Satan. If and when I do have an experience with a demon I am sure I will make an effort to report from a critical standpoint to offer support for the existence of this type of Biblical entity. But for now, I stand fast with my current experiences.

Sleep paralysis is a reality. It is experienced by many individuals, and thanks to researchers, people are able to come forward and share their experience without judgment or ridicule. This is the problem most people have in coming to terms with paranormal experiences. They simply don't want to be stigmatized and feel they must keep their stories to themselves. But most of all, they are hoping the frightening events of sleep paralysis will never happen again.

PART IV

R vs. LOVE

AL DECISION YOU'LL
NEED TO MAKE

LAX Airport 5901 W. Century Blvd., Los Angeles, CA 90045
tel: 310.215.6020 | fax: 310.491.7077

Huntington Park 5900 Pacific Blvd., Huntington Park, CA 90255
tel: 310.491.7080 | fax: 310.491.7081

Downtown LA 814 S. Francisco St., Los Angeles, CA 90017
tel: 310.491.7070 | fax: 310.491.7071

Montebello 2300 W. Beverly Blvd., Montebello, CA 90640
tel: 626.467.0202 | fax: 626.623.7625

FiFTEEn

Discovering Love

"The most wonderful of all things in life is the discovery of another human being with whom one's relationship has a growing depth, beauty, and joy as the years increase. This inner progressiveness of love between two human beings is a most marvelous thing; it cannot be found by looking for it or by passionately wishing for it. It is a sort of divine accident, and the most wonderful of all things in life."
SIR HUGH WALPOLE

"Where there is love there is life."
MAHATMA GANDHI

"Love and you shall be loved."
RALPH WALDO EMERSON

If there is no pleasure in love, then there is no love in pleasure. Think about this. We tend to believe love is a human emotion that is learned and developed throughout our lifespan. In reality it is the grandest essence of being human. We are born in love, and as we develop, we lose the concept of that love through the disheartening experiences that life produces. Ultimately we spend the rest of our lives trying to find the purity of this initial love because there is an ingrained need to have and to experience it again. Issues in early childhood preventing us from reconnecting with this purity of love may manifest themselves as maladaptive behavior later on in our lives.

Once a spirit enters the womb of the mother, the unborn child is in a state of unadulterated love. At birth, the spirit, with all its unconditional love, is trapped within the physical infantile body. With time, usually after the age of four, we rapidly lose our awareness of being a spirit. We develop a personality that is molded by our environment and adhere to it as we journey through life. During the growth process our spirit consciousness diminishes as our personality develops until we become spiritually ignorant. For some people this spiritual ignorance is reversed when they are able to receive information from spirit guides throughout their lives. When we become more sensitive to spirituality we evolve to a higher state of awareness to this love. Therefore, this state of love brings us to a co-consciousness with everything around us, which is a product of enlightenment or awareness.

After the age of four we become desensitized to the spirit world frequency from where we once came. During those first four years we are still in communication with the spirit world through spirit guides, who may come to us as imaginary friends. No one can see these spirit guides except children, encounters that parents usually discount as the product of their children's overactive imaginations.

Because we are spiritually sensitive in our early years, we are able to experience spirits without judging the encounters. As adults we learn to adjust to conceptual reasoning. As children we simply accept events for what they are and soon forget them unless the event is a traumatic experience stored in our subconscious mind.

I should mention here that many forms of childhood trauma have a tendency to embed fear, which is then processed much later in our adult lives. Insecurities such as low self-esteem are exacerbated and become a hindering factor in our relationships. Understanding how we think and why we react to certain situations in a negative manner can help us in the healing process to establish a healthy mental attitude toward expressing and accepting love.

It has been said, "With time we discover love." I would like to think we *rediscover* love. There are many ways to find love in our lives if it is love we are truly searching for. One may search throughout the world to find happiness from a person, an inanimate object, or a geographical location. The same exact person or object that makes you happy can also make you sad. Therefore, what we should strive for is to find inner joy, not short-lived happiness.

Joy brings the essence of love to us with the acceptance of all that comes our way. With joy we find the simple pleasures in life's fulfilling experiences, and we see the world with a fresh perspective. After we grow old with wisdom, we will find what we were looking for was always within us. When we go within, we find truth in unadulterated love and God's unconditional love. This introspection is where we will find meaning and fulfillment, which may help us to be balanced and joyful.

Spiritual joy is beyond ecstatic or exultant happiness; it is a state of acceptance regardless of prospects.

Relationships are one of the biggest concerns we have during our lifetime. There is one common experience every man and woman faces regardless of where they live on this planet: we all share and have experienced loneliness. One can still be in a state of loneliness even if surrounded by friends or family. It is this loneliness that brings us grief and sometimes depression. We are social beings, and science supports that this need is imprinted within us. In simplistic terms: we need to be loved.

I have encountered many people who have shared with me their feelings of loneliness. They claim their lives would be so much more fulfilling if they could only find someone to love and to spend time with. They really need to think about the reasons why they are feeling lonely and why they desire so much to be in love. I assure you the main reason they are in this state is due to a lack of self-love.

How can we love others if we do not love ourselves? People without self-love will likely spend most of their lives feeling empty within their relationships. In most cases they will be involved in relationships that were romantic in the beginning, yet with time diminish. For whatever reason, a person in such a relationship does not have a secure feeling of *self*. Because of this insecurity and lack of joy, this person may suffer from an internal disharmony, which in turn affects the relationship.

How can one break this cycle of bad relationships? First thing to consider, as mentioned earlier, is learning to love ourselves before we can love another. We can build purity and a sense of confidence by way of love, which can be shared with others unconditionally.

If we are lucky we will encounter the same purity in a life partner. If not, then we must accept the fact that if our partner does not realize the same concept of self-love, then the relationship will not work. Each individual will have to evolve to this concept, and it may be more difficult if the other person is not accepting of his or her own spiritual love.

One must accept that love cannot be forced upon others. By doing so the relationship is prone to failure. We have all spent wasted time on someone we think we can manipulate to fit our needs. You may simply have to move on instead of forcing it, and find joy within yourself until another person who was meant for you, your soul mate if you will, enters your life. Your soul mate is out there. You simply have to be free and secure, which in turn will cause attraction.

Every relationship should be considered an experience in how we see love, and we must learn from each and every one of these experiences. Remember that unconditional love doesn't mean you must stay with someone who is abusive or is unfaithful. These are negative expressions of love, which we should not accept into our environment. We must not engage in an unbalanced relationship when it comes to love. The abusive party can find another person to love negatively, only to find that the new partner will do the same.

We have more than one soul mate who may complement us. With time we will all cross paths with our soul mates through Spiritual Webbing. But we must first experience spiritual self-love.

We pray for God to bring someone into our lives because we *want* to be loved. God will grant what we ask, which is the state of *wanting* love. We will never actually *have* love from a person because we pray for God to keep us in the state of *wanting* love.

In other words, how can one *receive* love if one is asking to be in a state of *wanting* love? Therefore, reword your prayers, and thank God for what is coming as if it is already here. Give thanks for the life partner that is being sent to you through Spiritual Webbing.

Always remember there is no such thing as coincidence. It is the spirit world or the Creator's way of remaining anonymous, while still bringing you gifts. It has been thought by many that a "coincidence" is the spirit world throwing a pebble at you to offer you an experience that in some cases may be profound.

It is important to realize that your thoughts are powerful and creative, and they should be generated in a positive and loving way. Learn the aspect of inner peace and you will understand what I am trying to convey.

Is it possible when we pray we are establishing an affirmation? Are we possibly creating what we are asking for with prayer that is supported with intention? Is God simply remaining on the sidelines as a witness to what we are *creating* through prayer and manifesting on our own? I am in constant contemplation of these questions.

I feel nothing is ever etched in stone and regardless of how we feel about certain things or ideas they will always change as we evolve. Our belief systems dictate how we define our world. However, in reality we don't really know what benefits or harm will develop until we are affected by the very things we create. Therefore, our crucial responsibility to ourselves is to make love work in our lives. We are the creators of positive and negative experiences and are solely responsible for how we react to each — there are consequences.

All that we ask for is within our reach. But how we value material things compared to how we value love is the most important product of this teaching. When we truly do not have self-love, we do more things to punish ourselves and alienate people who love us. We choose to live a life of negativity because we have become accustomed to it. We consciously believe we are not deserving or capable of the purity of love.

Any form of addiction is an unconscious manifestation of something rooted in the subconscious mind. Addictions are based on some form of fear, where love is nonexistent. Addictions are a process of rehearsal, and with time become habits of the mind. In most cases addiction affects one's mental and physical health. It offers a false sense of comfort because it is familiar and it is constant.

Once we can pinpoint the reasons for an addiction, we can expose the fears that are at its foundation. When we replace fear with love, which we most definitely need to empower ourselves, it will give energy to combat the habitual act.

Many tools can be used other than traditional modern therapies. If the therapist is unconventional he/she may administer a holistic approach to addiction recovery, and one form of this nontraditional psychotherapy could be spiritual meditation.

Meditation is helpful in developing many aspects of mental and physical well-being. One such form is the practice of *Balík* Meditation and its complementary self-hypnosis, which is a focus technique.

I developed *Balík* Meditation to aid individuals in reaching a level of self-love so they may develop a state of bliss in which they can express unconditional love for themselves and for others. The core function of *Balík* Meditation is to connect the personality to the Spirit-self, bringing about a peaceful awareness of our true essence. It is a vehicle for transformation that is void of ego.

Whatever combination of tools is used, it must be based on the concept of unconditional self-love. Most importantly, one must know he/she can overcome and heal him- or herself from the agony and self-degradation of an addiction. Love overpowers fear, and the powerful use of thought can move mountains and create miracles in our lives.

Life produces many experiences that we can learn from, and one of the most profound is to understand the value of love for self, family, friends, and the community we live in. We can be the most successful person with all the material benefits that life can offer. However, when we die, we take nothing of the material world with us. When we are on our deathbed there is only one thing that we value the most — the love of family and the special people around us. We will reflect on the time we should have spent in loving our family instead of valuing the extra time spent at work to buy more things we thought would make us happier.

Try making a list of the negative aspects in your life, regardless of how small or large, and place them on the left side of a piece of paper. On the right side list the positive values that involve love either in the form of a person or an experience. Be honest in your listings. If your work comes up on the positive side, ask yourself if the time away from family is more valuable than time spent with them. If it is, then you may be a workaholic trying to find fulfillment outside of yourself.

Analyze the list you made but don't justify your intentions. Step away and look at the big picture. Only then will you learn that your life may need change, which will allow you to live in the presence of love and have fulfillment in your life.

When it comes to personal self-healing there is a technique I teach to my students of meditation. They practice it periodically in order to be responsible for their own lives.

Stand or sit in front of a mirror in a comfortable position and meditate for a few minutes. But before you do this, it is important to bless the mirror and yourself. The reason is it is possible for the mirror to be a portal for spirit entities. Therefore, protection and intention is important. Next, gaze into the mirror and picture yourself as a young child. You may even use a photograph of yourself in earlier years taped to the mirror to help visualize the child within. Once you can picture yourself in childhood when you were most vulnerable, take responsibility for healing the child you see in the mirror... do the things that are needed to save this child from whatever trauma was responsible for your depression or anxieties.

The power in this technique lies in the fact that many adults will not do for themselves what they will do for a child. This technique allows you to be a caretaker not only for yourself but for the child within who needs healing from traumas that were experienced during childhood. Forgiveness and acceptance is the key, and this is possible when we come to realize that we must take control.

People hate to be alone, and loneliness is painful, but we need to be alone so we are available for the one who is meant to share pure love with us. One way to fight the loneliness is to develop meditation techniques to aid in self-love in order to make us healthy mentally, emotionally, and spiritually. If we do this we will be prepared for the person who will come along to fulfill our desire for companionship, which is a necessity for humans. Love is an encounter of spiritual bliss that you have known before. In order to rediscover love, all you have to do is remember that it has always been within you.

If a crowd of people look at and attempt to identify what love means to each person, they will find love has many meanings. How one identifies love is how one will apply energy, sometimes useless energy, to formulate expectations upon others. It will be a design of the individual, and if this "designer" love is not reciprocated, one feels unloved. It is impossible to make someone love you, but it is possible for someone to see the love in you. Therefore, another person will reciprocate love by your example.

Is there truly a proper definition of love? As stated before, we all have our own concepts of what love should be, or at least what it means to us. Are there different levels of love? Absolutely, and one can argue that love varies depending on to whom it is being directed. One can say love is being patient, preserving the self, acting on trust, expressing affection, caring deeply, or simply being kind. Regardless of how love is measured or what emotion it conjures, it should be unconditional and purposeful.

The diverse meanings that love offers are complex as are the emotions that love can present. For some it is symbolic of interpersonal relationships and weighs heavily on psychological consequence. But the love that I am referring to is one that is encountered through self-discovery. This benevolence is attributed to the concept of self-love — not a narcissistic love. Spiritual love is what I am speaking of; it is void of ego, obsessive love, or any other form of false love. Self-love is primary for the individual to express interpersonal love for others in a wide sense that is positive, passionate, and most of all unconditional to support what many feel is the primary purpose of God's love.

In the book *The Seat of the Soul* (New York: Fireside, 1990), Gary Zukav writes:

> Spiritual partners are not together in order to quell each other's financial
> fears or because they can produce a house in the suburbs and that entire
> conceptual framework... The commitment of spiritual partners is to each
> other's spiritual growth, recognizing that that is what each of them is doing
> on Earth, and that everything serves that. (p. 125)

Consider you and your life partner as co-creators of a life of spiritual evolution
without expectations, and you will find joy in each other without the fear of aban-
donment or codependence. You really should not have to work hard for love. It is
right there within you. All one has to do is recognize it as a tool for growth, not as
a tool to hold another hostage.

SIXTEEN

The Power of Thought

"We are what we think. All that we are arises with our
thoughts. With our thoughts, we make our world."

BUDDHA

We all have the ability to control the circumstances of our experiences in life simply
because our thoughts empower us. We have the ability to overcome any negative
or traumatic experience if we understand the power of our thoughts. It becomes a
gift once we learn to tap into it during our spiritual evolution. This developmental
potential was designed for us before we were manifested in this earth realm in order
to evolve spiritually from each and every experience.

Our inner being has the ability to transform thought into a physical reality,
shaping the environment that we live in. Positive thoughts can be facilitated by first
visualizing the thought, vocalizing it out loud, and then placing it into action as a
creation of our own will. This is a very simple practice that offers great reward.

Within our religions we accept versions of truth based on faith. This approach to
truth prevents any form of critical thinking to challenge religious scripture or ideologies. We venture into life with a mindset that we are in control, when in reality we are
the ones being controlled. Therefore, we accept all that is either having its basis in religious faith or scientific theory. This directs the conscious mind towards a continuum in
supporting a given belief system that has been presented to us. Furthermore, a strong
belief diminishes any desire to question or venture outside of the current belief — no
thought processing needed.

A group or society may become dysfunctional in their thinking when adhering
to belief systems that invoke fear as a controlling tool, especially when used to limit
the awareness of its members. We are then at the mercy of others who construct the

belief system for us to enforce how we relate to the world around us. For example, if we continue to create fear through representations of "Good vs. Evil" mandated by organizations, religions, politics, or other ideologies, then we will continue to support the existence of evil as we give it energy. We will spend the rest of our lives fearing that which does not exist and is created by our own intention. With the idea of giving life to evil — we are in the presence of what we create. Therefore a given evil becomes a reality to its believers who choose to live in fear.

This is not to say that evil does not exist. This is merely an argument against the proclamation of "Good vs. Evil." German philosopher Friedrich Wilhelm Nietzsche (1844–1900) argues that the ideal human is capable of expressing passions in a creative way as opposed to suppressing them due to religious beliefs. He reasoned that believers, who are focused on the afterlife as proposed by Christianity, "the most fatal kind of self-presumption ever," are less capable of coping with their earthly life. Can we assume that fear is a deterrent to living a life free from evil? It depends on how we define good and evil, and its relationship to fear.

The proposition I make is to replace the concept of "Good vs. Evil" with "Love vs. Fear" as a beneficial thought process. This idea is a major theme throughout this book, and my wish is that my reader can see the value it offers and embrace it. As an example, I present to you a posting of an anonymous student who was present during one of my lectures given at California State University, Long Beach.

Good vs. Evil? Or Love vs. Fear?

Posted in Personal Blog by DragonKnight, November 3, 2004

During a presentation by the American Indian part of our Ethnic Experiences lectures (given by Richard Alaniz), I have been introduced to the concept of not believing in the concept of good and evil, but in the existence of love and fear.

So we take away base good and evil. Why? Because it objectifies things in which it becomes justified to destroy them or oppress. For example, American Indians were systematically slaughtered in an act of holocaust genocide of their people. All in the name of God. Why? Because they were barbarians who participated in "evil" acts. So the "good" of God's people is justified in the oppression of these primitive barbarians. The Crusades is another perfect example of one group of religious fanatics oppressing another in a disgusting act of bloodletting.

Now bring in fear and love. Evil does not beget fear... it is fear that begets the concept of evil. So when religious conservatives see something different, they fear it... then call it "evil" in order to objectify it as some kind of thing that must be defeated, subverted, and/or destroyed. So what is good? Good is another objectification (I sure hope that's an actual word) of something that must be worshipped, revered, and used to convert. But with love it becomes fluid as the concept of love is not to objectify, but to give freely. With good and evil we tend to solidify things so that we can easily justify one's actions even though it may hurt another. But with fear we can define why something bad is happening without simply saying they are evil. With love we can define why we help others openly without using the excuse that we are doing just good.

I like this concept of love and fear. It gives us a better opportunity for becoming more open-minded to the other side rather than just our own. For the concepts of good and evil take sides. Love and fear is in everything. With that in mind, we can come to a better understanding not only [of] one another… but of ourselves as well.

He undoubtedly absorbed what my lecture offered. He eloquently states how nations and individuals can misrepresent ideologies when applying the construct of good and evil. When one replaces the concept of "Good vs. Evil" with "Love vs. Fear" one can analyze any behavior and determine if the action is a representation of love or fear.

We are conditioned to "thought limitations," we accept what we are directed to accept by institutions or people of authority. It is this perpetuated "thought limitation" that holds us prisoners to the status quo without any desire for further investigation.

Our knowledge relies on science, which analyzes our physical world. The problem is, not "all" science is completely objective as it claims to be. At times it is subjective due to personal ideas, ego, politics, and the parameters established by science using language to reason with its findings. This is not to claim that science is unworthy or useless; on the contrary, it serves us well. I make the claim that behavioral science, in some cases, expresses an "innocent ignorance" that makes it limited when it comes to the paranormal or multidimensional entities.

The established scientific mindset devalues paranormal events, but to truly be objective, science must approach the possibilities seriously to develop measurable techniques that will allow scientists to venture into a new frontier. It is important to consider spirituality, not in a religious context, but as an extension of mankind's experience — spirituality should be approached in a scientific manner.

Bidirectional interaction of science and mysticism involving consciousness concepts may unleash the shackles that bind us when addressing the paranormal. Great minds understand realities beyond what we can physically measure within our current science; one such person today is Deepak Chopra, MD.

I found the debate *"The Great Afterlife"* between Dr. Chopra (arguing for consciousness beyond death) and Dr. Michael Shermer (relying on science as the all-knowing debunker of the paranormal and life after death) very interesting. Both are intellectuals and their arguments are reasonable. However, to establish a definitive "winner" in this debate is to fall victim to the saying, "it depends on one's preconceived beliefs." What amazed me was the intelligence and resources used by each to support his argument; but the audience was still left with previous beliefs or skepticism. My personal experiences support Dr. Chopra's argument. I admire his ability to argue and support his theory with science — a very hard task indeed.

Although I *know* there is life after death, due to my explicit experiences, I am incapable of proving it scientifically. Dr. Chopra has greater resources and intelligence than most in attempting to challenge the entrenched scientific community that harbors skeptics. In time he will succeed, and the benefactors will be humanity.

Negative or positive thoughts are what create a disturbed or balanced expression of life. It is said, "It is as *you* see it." Depression and other mental disorders can be altered with cognitive techniques of the Psychospiritual perspective. It offers tools to help *you* change *your* mind in how you relate to your life issues.

Biopsychologists, who use various neuropsychological tests to assess brain functions and structure, have found the human brain contains endless possibilities and capabilities. Redundancy (parallel processing) and plasticity (capacity for continuous alterations) are terms used by biopsychologists for brain functions. Their consideration at this time is there are "unused" or "underdeveloped" areas of the brain — undiscovered territory.

We still have much to learn about how we think and how the mind is intertwined with the brain. However, I feel there is no special consideration for the healing capabilities of our thoughts when it comes to scientific research for understanding the interactions of the mind and brain. Modern psychology considers any metaphysical ideology to be taboo and sidesteps it out of concern for maintaining scientific reputability. Conservative scientists, who adhere to archaic theories of psychology, ridicule metaphysical psychological studies.

Cognitive psychologists study a computer's artificial intelligence to aid them in finding how computers process information similarly to the human brain. Because both operate on information processing and rules, cognitive psychologists claim, "The mind is to the brain as software is to hardware." But they are missing an important aspect of the *source*. The operational source of a computer is plugged into a wall circuit, but where do humans receive their source?

The idea of identifying a human's source falls into the philosophical realm that encompasses all of the outer layers of science. Anything that cannot be observed with the scientific method is considered a philosophical idea and is relegated to that category. However, within the martial sciences, masters are familiar with an inner source referred to as *Chí*, described as life force energy.

When practicing *Balík* Meditation techniques, one can learn how to develop *Chí* flow. When used in tandem with thoughts and affirmations there is a potential of healing for better physical and psychological wellness. This meditation can allow one to reach a higher state of consciousness. Through constant practice, we may find ourselves within a "zone" or "gap" that enables awareness and possible communication with multidimensional sources as guides to a higher state of consciousness.

According to British philosopher Alan Watts (1915–73), thinking is a complex act. It is a manipulation of symbols, "whether they be words, numbers or signs such as triangles, squares, circles, astrological signs, or whatever... to represent events that are going on in the real world is what I call thinking."

William James (1842–1910), an American philosopher, defined true beliefs for most people as "beliefs that are useful to the believer." He added a dimension to the theory of truth as pieces of a puzzle that fit together. James, favoring pragmatism, "true for him who experiences the workings," felt that individual truth was dependent upon its use and function for the person who held to that truth. Part of this pragmatism was the application of what he called "radical empiricism" in that "truth emerges from diverse experiences interpreted as facts."

Experience, as James sees it, has "sense data" as content and a reference. He concluded that truths disclosed by the mystic are "only true for the mystic." These truths are to be contemplated but cannot be truth for others unless it is experienced personally. He further states that "transempirical entities may exist, but that it's not fruitful to talk about them."

To be a cognitive miser is to circumvent the process of having to think. We simply apply our prejudices and current beliefs so we don't have to waste energy on critical thinking. It is easier and takes less time, but is prone to error. In understanding the *Power of Thought* we must first give consideration to how we think as well as the mechanics of thought processing. If we can remember to be responsible for our thoughts because they will affect others, then perhaps we can produce a positive approach to relating to others, void of negativity and prejudices.

Awakening Through the Gap

"For as long as you direct your search to the forms around you, you will not attain your goal even after aeon upon aeon; whereas, by contemplating your inner awareness, you can achieve Buddhahood in a single flash of thought."

CH'AN MASTER HUI HAI
ZEN TEACHING OF INSTANTANEOUS AWAKENING

Religious spirituality is supported by faith, faith is supported by belief, and belief is persistent through tenacity. On the contrary, I feel we are not supposed to have total faith in our beliefs; we are to question our beliefs through our experiences, which is the path to awareness. And this can only happen when one is in a state of *knowing*. A belief system is one's worst enemy… it gets in the way of truth. You will be unable to become aware if you are afraid to break from a set of ideas designed by others represented as a belief system.

In Deepak Chopra's book *Synchrodestiny*, he refers to a quantum gap concept and applies detailed information about a gap within existence. He uses the example of film in what he calls the "frame-and-gap sequence of a motion picture."

The example of a motion picture is used to represent the "gap" that separates each frame. When put in motion the frames produce a picture that we accept as reality. The gap as described by Chopra is the point in between all actions, all thoughts, all existence of reality. It is where one event ends and the next one begins. According to quantum physicists, this is how our world exists.

We are busy living in the "real world" with our daily routine and logically accept the idea that there is nothing more than what we see. But unlike the mystic, most people don't focus on the in-between state that I refer to as the realm of awareness. This realm, space that harbors information and knowledge, is where we can experience a psychic expression of reality. This fissure or gap holds the truth to spirit consciousness and allows one to experience a separate reality. Therefore, every physical element —including thought — is not solid matter; it consists mostly of space — more precisely gaps — as a byproduct of materialistic energy.

As I see it, this is the "gap of creation" where thoughts are creative, effects of prayers are manifested, and where we create our highest potential. In my experience in shamanism this "gap of creation" is where evolved shamans and healers dwell in indigenous societies to perform healings. Not all shamans have this intuitive gift or spiritual knowledge. However, this knowledge has been known for centuries.

Within our accepted reality there are many gaps in every moment of our living being. Once we are in the gap or realm of awareness, we can experience a higher awareness. The tool of meditation can help place us in this realm to reach a higher level of consciousness and ultimately a true awakening.

Meditation has been used by many cultures to achieve higher states of consciousness. However, we cannot do this if we are preoccupied with things outside of one's true self. We need to look within our spiritual self to learn to focus, to listen, to feel, and then to experience reality.

While in meditation one utilizes relaxation and cultivates inner focus thereby allowing one to contemplate what is internal. Once awareness is achieved, we learn to bypass our third-dimensional realities to reach a higher consciousness, which induces an awakening to truth. There are many dimensions that exist at the same time, which harbor realities beyond our current comprehension. However, mystics have dwelled there for centuries and have gained knowledge that science has yet to uncover. In the future, I feel the science of theoretical physics will include mysticism and ancient wisdom.

To experience an awakening is to reach the fullest potential of knowing who you really are — a spirit. Siddhartha Gautama (Buddha) ascended to the level of Buddhahood when he reached the state of awakening. According to Buddhist teachings, everyone is capable of reaching enlightenment and becoming a Buddha. This awareness that I am talking of is giving attention to the ultimate you; it is subtle energy that allows one to realize spirit consciousness within what organismic theorist Kurt Goldstein refers to as self-actualization, a term Goldstein originally introduced. Where do we find this? We find it when we experience the in-betweenness, the realm of creation, the area of the unknown, the gap or void between everything and all things. The term self-actualization has been used within various psychology theories and in different ways by Abraham Maslow, Carl Rogers, and other psychologists.

When we are aware of our own Spirit-self we are centered in peace and in a knowing of the unknown, the underlying intelligence of the physical world. We relinquish all that is negative to create a harmonious space of creative love, which is the true self of mind, body, and spirit. It is a feeling of bliss that words cannot describe. You have been there before in many incarnations, and the ultimate goal is to reach a higher state of awareness with each time you are incarnated.

Our cultural and social beliefs teach us that we are limited in our human potential; we do not play a part in our creative potential outside of our personalities, the work that we do, the societies we build. The real potential is in how we are able to be creative, not only to affect our experiences using the creative mind, but mostly to create the ability to connect to universal truth. How do we learn to do this? One way is to achieve it through focused energy that is unaffected by the external world — meditation.

While in the stillness of the conscious subtle mind we may have an experience that is foreign to us. This feeling is beyond our five senses. With time and practice it becomes familiar because we are learning to connect — we are in the realm of awareness — in communion with the spirit world.

Directed meditation is used to cleanse the mind, if even for a moment, of our daily routine in order to open a door to an existence that is unfamiliar. We are focused on experiencing a clean silence that is innocent of our intelligence, ego, and is free from the static of everyday thought occurrences. While meditating, ask yourself if you are truly in a state of meditation or if your mind is drifting and is enhanced by your imagination. If you answer, "Yes, I am drifting," then simply acknowledge the noise or chatter and move toward focusing your attention back to your meditation. By acknowledging everything that presents itself without trying to manipulate or control it you are freeing yourself from thought energy and will be able to re-focus.

Look for clarity and see if your personality has changed with the practice of meditation. Continue to ask yourself key questions. Do others see a difference in me? Do I react to life stressors differently than before? Do I feel more enriched in how I think and am I distancing myself from previous beliefs? If you answer, "Yes," then you are evolving and have had guidance through your meditations. You will find you are in a new perspective free of the assumption that you are not in control.

Enlightenment is a catchphrase some people use to fulfill their ego to represent themselves as somehow "better" or "purer" when in reality enlightenment should be void of ego. The road to enlightenment is the reduction of the ego; it is when you find yourself connected, not disconnected, to others. You will find no specific energy powers or magical powers of the physical world in someone who is truly enlightened. They are in *oneness* with everything around them and have no need for power.

The product of enlightenment and its realization is *knowing.* Knowing is an experience of truth and void of any title unless you use the term "all-knowing" which is referring to the Godhead. There are no powers or mystical energies allocated to knowing. It is a perceptive indulgence and authentication, not a level or rank that separates you from everyone else.

Truth can allow you to function in a stressful world. If you accept the truth, you can have a fulfilling life. Do not allow your growth to be sabotaged by social constructs or by what society says is conventional. If you do, you are in jeopardy of remaining stagnant and could simply find another belief system to attach yourself to. This in turn will be passed on to your children and their children as tenaciously as it has been for eons.

We have two minds that are categorically separate: the conscious mind and the subconscious mind (sometimes referred to as the unconscious mind). The conscious mind is aware of information and actions you are focused on at the moment; it is responsible for logic and reasoning. The subconscious mind, or unconscious mind, is aware of what you are not focused on and can be expressed without your knowing it.

The subconscious mind influences your beliefs, your behaviors, your unconscious skills, unconscious thoughts, your habits, and phobias to name a few. These subconscious behaviors are influenced and based on your environment. It is the functional part generating your emotions. It is also a motivator of your desires and a storehouse of your childhood experiences, good and bad.

The conscious mind is your thinking mind that is registering and processing information. It analyzes everyday data and experiences in a logical manner. With time, information decays and is forgotten unless it is rehearsed. It lives in the moment but can become memory and will surface when called upon. Information from the conscious mind is mechanically processed and is then transferred where it can be either stored as short-term or long-term memory. It is usually information within the conscious mind that we are interested in or will use repeatedly in our daily lives. We have a tendency not to focus on the effects of the subconscious mind. However, it is the culprit behind hidden agendas that are played out throughout our lives.

Now that we have a general understanding of cognition, we can identify a separate category: spirit consciousness. When you are in acceptance due to an epiphany or a profound experience, you are in an understanding of spirit consciousness. You will not need years of meditation to be enlightened. You will have already broken the bonds of the conscious mind to unleash spirit-conscious freedom. You will not have to go anywhere special or follow anyone for the truth. You will know it when you know it. It is a feeling that I cannot explain with words. You will make a contact that no one can define; it will be awareness that only you can recognize as viable.

When we experience an epiphany or a profound spiritual experience, it is as if our Spirit-self is being confirmed. We are vitalized with this confirmation. We will feel "at home" because this is where we have come from. We are in a state of remembering.

To understand the concept of awakening through the gap one must read and study this idea from more than one source. I do not have all the answers nor do I tell it in a manner that everyone can understand. Therefore, I suggest reading various books on spirituality that convey concepts of the gap or realm of awareness so you can have various perspectives and perhaps find a common thread.

As spirituality is both simplistic and complex, it is important to research as many perspectives until you find language and ideas that fit your understanding. Like anything else, it is a process and is very rewarding once you reach a higher level of awareness.

You will come to a moment of realization and will have reached a greater truth. Within that realization you will have a sense of triumph in reaching your final destination of enlightenment through awareness.

An awakening is a homecoming. It is an expression of your potentiality and an understanding without the use of dialog or symbols. An awakening is void of ego — your personality, which is not the real you, falls away. It is a reality separate from a space-time that you have been conditioned to accept and will learn eventually of its illusory properties. It is a connection to all that is, an insight into essential wholeness — a perfect union with the Godhead. Within the moment of awakening there exist no mysteries, and one will find there is no longer a need to achieve — you are in true bliss and within a *knowing* that you have arrived.

Regardless of which term or exotic catchphrase is used to describe awakening through the gap, it is an essential component in understanding how we are supposed to connect to the concept of our spiritual self. How do we know when we are within the gap? In simple terms it is within itself an expression of total awareness, the ultimate *aha* moment of discovery that is tangible — an elation of being and a celebration of beauty and belonging. Once appreciated, we are no longer in a state of ignorance. Clarity is exponentially revived — we have awakened — we are now the Buddha.

Tipping Point to Awareness

"The tipping point is that magic moment when an idea, trend, or
social behavior crosses a threshold, tips, and spreads like wildfire."
MALCOLM GLADWELL

"In a time of deception, telling the TRUTH is an act of revolution."
GEORGE ORWELL

I have found more people who are now coming to accept the possibility that they
are a continuum of life energy that is void of death and are to advance with each
lifetime to a higher spiritual consciousness. I am not alone in understanding there *is*
consciousness after death — many others know this to be true.

We are learning that happiness is short-lived, but *joy* is forever. Material things
come and go, but joy makes the inner soul rich. And if we feel hopelessness at any
time in our lives, we always know that someone else is suffering even more greatly.

War no longer represents patriotism as strongly as it once did. People are becoming
more aware of war's pitfalls; it is no longer as beneficial to the advancement of our
culture. We have witnessed that war only serves a few who profit from it, and as we
learn which demographic groups of people disproportionately suffer loss of life and
limb from war, we find they are our neighbors and our sons and daughters.

If we do not send our children to the battlefield there will not be anyone to fight
a war. The politicians and financiers will not bear arms to fight for their personal
agendas. It is your children they choose to sacrifice. Present to me a list of elite
bankers and elite corporate heads whose children were sacrificed for their wars.
There is no such list.

Those in power use patriotism, politics, and religious dogma to induce fear by
creating an enemy who they say is threatening your freedom only to gain more

financial power through war. I was naive to think that it would end with the Vietnam War — it didn't, and we have had two wars at the time of this writing in 2013, Afghanistan and Iraq, to continue what we didn't learn with Vietnam.

The average American did not realize that the operative word, "communism," was used to keep us in *fear* and was a term promoted by the media as an excuse to go to war in Vietnam. The U.S. lost over 58,000 lives because of the feared "Domino Effect," which was being repeated by political warmongers to induce fear in the general public. At the time of this writing, it is 2013, and America has been conducting business for many years with China and Vietnam who still define themselves as communist nations — so much for the "evils" of communism when a profit can be made. Today, the operative word is "terrorism," and I am sure that in time we will find this threat was not as it was preached. On the contrary, some nations see America as a terrorist threat to their way of life, thereby causing terrorist reprisal.

Greater amounts of people are discovering inner peace by the practice of meditation and are finding it is a tool for self-discovery and a means to gain a different awareness, ultimately reaching a higher consciousness. They are learning to advance their lives to a state of spiritual and mental balance.

We are truly experiencing a revolution at this time — a spiritual revolution. We are coming to know a truth that is not constricted by previous beliefs as we apply ourselves to investigate our experiences that are outside of the norm. We have found that our limitations were due to how we were conditioned to believe. To advance our human potential we have found it is OK to break the mold of our current beliefs.

Much of how we view the world is based on theory and speculation. We as a society have a tendency to not value what many actually experience. We discount viable reports given by large numbers of people and at times label their expression as mass hysteria.

Many historical personalities, such as scientists Galileo Galilei and Alfred Wegener, were outliers who brought gifts of knowledge to the world. Only after time passed did their theories find enough acceptance to benefit humankind in conventional terms. Only after death were they seen as geniuses. Prior to that, they were stigmatized as eccentric, skewed, or perhaps even mad for possessing such obscene and confounded ideologies. Perhaps as a progressive society we will allocate energy to investigate new ideologies; they could possibly hold the key that may unlock mysteries.

The "tipping point" is a phrase coined by Morton M. Grodzins, a professor of political science, who studied the movement of whites from a community once a given percentage of African-American families moved into their neighborhoods. This point of social exodus by whites was known as "white flight" once the moment of tipping point was reached.

Malcolm Gladwell's book *The Tipping Point: How Little Things Can Make a Big Difference* (New York: Little, Brown, 2000) popularized the phrase "tipping point" which is now used so frequently it has become a common cliché. Gladwell described the "tipping point" as the moment in time when a given percentage of the population finds an event or idea popular enough to cause interest within the remaining population. Once the tipping point is reached, the idea will permeate throughout the society.

Right now, a shared connectedness is contagious and is gradually permeating globally. We are reaching a tipping point as groups of like-minded individuals come to an awareness of spirituality outside of religious dogma. I feel that in the imminent future, science will be at the threshold of spirituality, and its stakeholders will hopefully be motivated to develop theories for further spiritual discovery outside of popular religious tenets.

We are at the brink of universal acceptance that extraterrestrials are and have been a part of the human experience. A multitude of people are beginning to question their governments about the evidence of extraterrestrial existence. They no longer accept labels of "mass hysteria" to define what they have witnessed and are seriously investigating the claims of others.

The youth are coming to a realization that their parents' belief systems do not satisfy their personal quest for knowledge. Young people use the Internet to discover information on their own terms if they learn to research and decipher fact from misinformation. There are concerns that in the near future some institutions or perhaps corporations may have interest in controlling the Internet. Why would that be? Control the ability of the people to share new ideas and you control the minds of the population.

When we separate ourselves from another group we label them as "different," and therefore relate to each other as "us against them." Separatism is brought about when a specific group or religion claims to own the absolute truth and will diligently protect that idea. Perhaps it is better to acknowledge that each religion interprets a piece of the truth, thereby uniting us all as one.

We are beginning to step outside of our previous beliefs and are advancing to a new perspective that is void of fear. I am talking about a perspective that does not support war, greed, dehumanization of people, or destruction of a culture because it is different from our own.

We are finding that as we are busy working harder in order to keep up with society as defined by corporations we are spending less time with our families, which will cause us to lose control of our children. This is what modern societies have been conditioned to buy into. The solution is simple; do not consume products that you really don't need. Turn off your televisions, and "tune into" your families.

The key to your survival is to understand the true meaning of love and how to manifest it in every action and thought. Learn to think outside of the labels that have been given to you as a function of your everyday thinking (e.g., liberal/conservative, Republican/Democrat, Christian/Muslim, rich/poor, us/them), and you will find yourself in a different mindset. You will learn to practice critical thinking skills in reaching your own conclusions without being controlled by a belief system or the manipulation of "talking heads" who are paid millions by corporations to control your thinking and beliefs with misinformation and logical fallacies.

What I offer is for you to learn to live by being compassionate and to find the truth in order to advance to your full human potential. Seek life gracefully by living fully and choosing love over fear. My friends, this is the path to God Consciousness.

We are in a new age of awareness. We are at the brink of another "tipping point" in which we can redesign our reality. By doing so, we will value a world that favors peace, love, and God Consciousness instead of greed, ego, and war. We must replace "Good vs. Evil" with "Love vs. Fear" as each individual's path to awareness as co-creators. Personal thought is where I create my world, and in these thoughts reside love or fear... *I choose Love.*

Glossary

agnostic: A person who believes it is impossible to know or prove that God exists

atheist: A person who is skeptical of supernatural claims and believes there is no existence of deities. The term atheism is a Greek word (*atheos*), meaning "without god."

Balík Meditation: A meditative practice developed by *Guro* Richard L. Alaniz to help others awaken their spiritual awareness by channeling *Chí* through focused dynamic breathing, isometric postures, and enhanced mental awareness to further one's spiritual consciousness.

brujo: An indigenous practitioner who uses incantations to invoke spirits as well as cast spells

Chí: Also known as "*Qi.*" A Chinese term meaning "internal life force energy." *Chí* is used within many traditional Chinese medicinal healing and martial arts disciplines.

cognitive miser: A person who uses limited information or thinking as a cognitve shortcut to arrive at a decision, eliminating relevant information.

cold readings: A technique used by psychics and others to read information about a person without prior knowledge

critical thinking: According to the author, to think critically is not to approve or disapprove. It is an examination of evidence, assumptions, values, and reflection to evaluate credibility outside of one's prejudices, emotions, social ideologies, beliefs, and imposed stigmas.

curandero: Rooted in indigenous cultures in Mexico, meaning "spiritual healer." A *curandero* will use herbs and connect to spirits to bring about a healing and in some instances will credit Jesus Christ for their healing power. *Curandero* should not be confused with *brujo.*

déjà vu: A French expression meaning "already seen." A feeling of having experienced some event before. The term was coined by Émile Boirac (1851–1917), a French psychic researcher.

developmental potential: The potentiality of each individual to develop spiritually in order to reach a higher spiritual consciousness

DSM-IV-TR: The fourth edition (2000) of the *Diagnostic and Statistical Manual of Mental Disorders*, a publication by the American Psychiatric Association, which provides standard classification of mental disorders

Divine Intervention: An active involvement by a Higher Being with humans to enhance spiritual potential

Earth guide: A human's role as an Earth Angel whose purpose is to help others to become aware of their spiritual potential

facilitated communication: A term used by the author to describe how spirit guides employ telepathy or thought implanting to those who they are guiding

generative fathering: A commitment to work toward proper caring for the next generation of children

hypnotic suggestion: A phenomenon where a perception can be programmed usually when one is under hypnosis. Events or behavioral actions can be achieved by suggestion, or a set of keywords that when suggested can trigger a given response.

ideomotor effect: A psychological phenomenon where unconscious motions are made by a subject as in a reflexive action to pain. For example, tears are released due to a reaction to an intense emotion.

Induced Knowledge: A term used by the author to represent spiritual knowledge given by a higher source, it is a pure representation of *knowing*.

introspection: A reflective inward self-examination of one's own deep thoughts, feelings, and sensations

karma: Originating in ancient India, an Eastern religious concept of "the law of cause and effect," where one's actions in this life or previous lives are a cycle of cause and effect in the next life

Karmonic Experience: A term coined by the author to describe how one's life-plan experiences were designed before one incarnates to fulfill one's spiritual evolution to spiritual awareness

Ki: A term used in Japan to represent *Chi* (internal life force energy)

know vs. believe: Used by the author and others to bring attention to the differences of each, as most use these terms interchangeably to represent the same meaning. Many use the term "I believe" when communicating an idea as a representation of an absolute as if they "know" it to be true when in reality they have not experienced it for themselves.

Love vs. Fear: Described by the author as a superior representation of human dynamics, and is argued by him that "Love vs. Fear" should replace the battle of

"Good vs. Evil" as this current human ideology is problematic for human potential. If a person can see an action as either stemming from love or fear, instead of being good or evil, then one can readjust his or her perspective and reaction to the event or idea.

Mana: A term used in Hawaii to represent *Chí* (internal life force energy)

medium: Also known as psychic medium, a person who has the ability to communicate with the spirit of one who has passed to the other world or with agents of other dimensions

mescal: Mescal or mezcal comes from the Nahautl words *metl* and *ixcalli* meaning "oven-cooked agave." The Mescalero Apaches received their name from the Mexicans because the Apaches were known to eat the leaves of the agave/mescal plant after baking them.

metaphysics: Derives from the Greek words *metá,* meaning ("beyond" or "after") and *physiká* (physics), which is not easily defined. Metaphysical philosophy examines the nature of what exists.

miracle: An event that is unexplainable by the laws of nature and is therefore considered supernatural or an act of God

Moving Beyond Belief Systems: According to the author, a need for societies to move away from current, tenaciously held beliefs that have historically been responsible for the bloodletting of innocent people and the demise of cultures, due to the need of individuals or groups to force their beliefs on others. A belief is not a truth, it is an idea that is supported with faith and is represented as truth to achieve a specific agenda.

multidimensional: Having more than one dimension that is measurable or based on mathematics or theory. The author uses the term to represent a property of space and an extension in time to infer there is a spiritual dimension.

mysticism: From the Greek word *mystikos,* a system of knowledge or practice that includes a state of consciousness that is beyond the current acceptable perception of human awareness.

mythology: The interpretation of a body of myths belonging to a culture depicting their history, heroes, gods, and supernatural beings.

omen: A prophetic sign or foretelling of an outcome supposedly from either good or evil. According to the author, a sign is a physical representation of an omen.

orb: The simplest form of a disembodied spirit taking the form of a ball of light energy *paranormal:* Derived from the Latin prefix "para" meaning "against, counter, outside or beyond the norm." Paranormal events are phenomena that are beyond the acceptable normal scientific explanation of reality.

past life regression: In a psychotherapeutic setting hypnosis is used to recover memories of past life experiences.

past life/reincarnation: The return of a spirit or soul after death or transition to the spirit world, rebirthed within a newborn. The idea of rebirth or reincarnation is common in Buddhism, Hinduism, Jainism, and Sikhism, and is found within the ideas of Greek philosophers.

Prana: A term used in India to represent *Chí* (internal life force energy)

premonition: From the Latin word *praemonitus,* meaning to forewarn, a paranormal warning by way of a cognitive conscious feeling of an impending future event. Symbolic lucid dreams are often premonitions.

psychic: From the Greek word *psychikos* meaning "of mind, mental," a person who has extrasensory perception and is able to perceive information outside of normal senses

Psychospiritual Psychology: An applied psychological model developed by the author after many years as an apprentice shaman and an education in psychology. This model includes the synthesis of indigenous shamanism and modern psychological theories such as Gestalt and psychodrama therapy.

puberty ritual: An ancient practice of the Mescalero Apache of New Mexico as a rite of passage to womanhood by young Apache maidens once they reach puberty, and represents the central aspect of Apache religious practice

radical empiricism: Developed by William James (1842–1910), an American psychologist, a pragmatist doctrine that defines relationships of particulars to explain physical levels of one's experiences, and goes beyond scientific empiricism. A combination of natural senses (visual, hearing, sensation, taste, and smell) is justifiable in supporting what one experiences.

realm of awareness: A state of total awareness outside of our four-dimensional reality. It is an experience in a higher reality that is a condition of transitioning to another dimension outside of what we are used to.

separatism: A belief or a movement for a separation from others across any one of a combination of various divisions, including politics, race, religion, geography, cultures, communities, or beliefs *shadow people:* Supernatural dark entity humanoid figures that appear in dark silhouette form and are at times seen through one's peripheral vision. According to paranormal popular culture shadow people come in various forms and harbor malevolent intention. For more information on shadow people read the first book written on the subject, *The Secret War* by Heidi Hollis, *www.heidihollis.com.*

sign: An event of significance designed to elicit a response or to inform; an omen.

sleep paralysis: A paranormal event that occurs when one either is waking up or just before one falls asleep. Many report feeling a sensation of being paralyzed for a brief moment. During the event one feels as if someone or something is in the room observing him or her with a malevolent intent.

spirit consciousness: Used by the author to depict conscious awareness of the Spirit-self and spiritual realm, outside of that which is described by current religious ideologies

spiritual evolution: A personal spiritual growth process by which each experience, paranormal or not, allows a person to evolve to a higher consciousness to reach one's awareness to spirituality

Spiritual Webbing: Concept that many people are brought into your life to help guide you to a higher awareness

thought limitations: Restrictions in one's ability to advance to an extended thought process usually due to level of information, knowledge, or of one being a "cognitive miser," meaning one prefers to subscribe to tenaciously held beliefs, social stigmas, social biases, and preconceived prejudices instead of advancing to critical thinking

vortex: A spiraling motion around a center of air or water as it rotates. In Sedona, Arizona, a vortex is identified as a multidimensional spiraling spiritual energy location where people meditate for prayer and healing.

X-Ops: A paranormal reality pilot program filmed in 2005 for the Discovery Channel. Mr. Alaniz and seven other experts in various fields investigated paranormal activity in Roswell, New Mexico's UFO museum, rehab center, and Hangar 84. Discovery Channel (DC) refused to release it to the public after investing $300,000 in the production. One theory is that the government put pressure on DC not to air the program since the X-Ops team encountered a multidimensional entity as well as other paranormal activity using scientific equipment in real time, all caught on film.

Bibliography

Brainy Quote. www.brainyquote.com. Retrieved January 15, 2010.

Brodd, Jefferey. *World Religions*. Winona, MN: Saint Mary's Press, 2003.

Bryant, Edwin H. *Krishna: A Sourcebook*. New York: Oxford University Press, 2007.

Cheyne, A. J., Newby-Clark, I.R., & Rueffer, S.D. *Sleep Paralysis and Associated Hypnagogic and Hypnopompic Experiences*. Journal of Sleep Research, 8, 313-318 (1999).

Chopra, Deepak. *Synchrodestiny: Harnessing the Infinite Power of Coincidence to Create Miracles*. New York: Random House, 2005.

Clark, Stephen R. L. *World Religions and World Order*. Religious Studies, 26.1, 1990.

Cohen, Joan Lebold. *Buddha*. New York: Delacorte Press, 1969.

Gladwell, Malcolm. *The Tipping Point: How Little Things Can Make a Big Difference*. New York: Little, Brown, 2000.

Grodzins, Morton M. *The Metropolitan Area as a Racial Problem*. Pittsburgh: University of Pittsburgh Press, 1958.

Holy Bible: New Living Translation. Wheaton, IL: Tyndale House Publishers, Inc., 1996.

James, William. *Essays in Radical Empiricism (1912)*. Mineola, NY: Dover Publications, 2003.

Jewish Virtual Library. www.jewishvirtuallibrary.org/jsource/biography/moses.html. Retrieved June 1, 2010.

Jung, Carl. *Synchronicity: An Acausal Connecting Principle*. New York: Routledge and Kegan Paul, 1972.

Nietzsche, Friedrich. *Beyond Good and Evil*. Translation by Walter Kaufmann. New York: Random House, 1966.

Robinson, Richard H., Johnson, Willard L. *The Buddhist Religion*. Belmont, CA: Wadsworth Publishing, 1997.

Rodinson, Maxime. *Muhammad: Prophet of Islam*. New York: The New Press, 2002.

Rosen, Steven. *Essential Hinduism*. Westport, CN: Praeger, 2006.

Satsvarupa dasa Goswami. *The Qualities of Sri Krsna*. LaCrosse, FL: GNPress, 1995.

Telushkin, Rabbi Joseph. *Jewish Literacy*. New York: William Morrow and Co., 1991.

Tishken, Joel E. *Ethnic vs. Evangelical Religions: Beyond Teaching the World Religion Approach*. The History Teacher 33.3, 2000.

Tolle, Eckhart. *A New Earth: Awakening to Your Life's Purpose*. New York: Plume, 2005.

Watts, Alan. *The Philosophies of Asia*. North Clarendon, VT: Tuttle Publishing, 1995.

Zukav, Gary. *The Seat of the Soul*. New York: Fireside/Simon & Schuster, 1990.

About the Author

Richard Alaniz received his B.A. degree in psychology from California State University Long Beach and has over twenty-five years of training in indigenous shamanic practices. He has lectured at various universities in Southern California on indigenous spiritual healing practices. When not lecturing he is a writer/researcher, meditation teacher, and a spiritual counselor incorporating modern psychological theories and indigenous shamanic principles.

Over the course of Mr. Alaniz's sixteen-year practice as a spiritual counselor he developed a new paradigm in approaching psychology, which he calls Psychospiritual Psychology. This new approach to therapy involves the process of spirit consciousness, which aids clients to gain awareness of what he calls the Spirit-self, in order to bring about a positive outcome within the counseling process.

With over thirty-five years of training in various martial arts, Mr. Alaniz has earned the title of *Punong Guro* (Principal Master) of *Balík Kali Silat* martial arts. With his comprehensive knowledge he developed *Balík* Meditation as a means to guide participants to spiritual consciousness and physiological wellness. He is currently completing *Balík Meditation: Wellness to Mind-Body-Spirit*, a how-to book on meditation and good health for all ages. His method of meditation is an easy step-by-step process designed to connect the personality to the Spirit-self to induce spiritual awareness for wellness in one's life.

Mr Alaniz's public speaking events have helped many people engage in their own transformation to inner peace and awareness. His lectures expose the detrimental effects of the ego and belief systems that condition individuals to evade spiritual consciousness, which in turn contributes to false perspectives and attitudes affecting families, communities, and social structures.

www.balikinstitute.com

Balík INSTITUTE
Wellness to Mind-Body-Spirit

Richard Alaniz is committed to directing others towards a higher spiritual consciousness, awareness, and wellness to mind-body-spirit through lectures, seminars, clinics, and book clubs. Mr. Alaniz is available to serve your needs in small or large forums. He may be contacted at the official *Balík* Institute website:

www.balikinstitute.com
balikinstitute@hotmail.com

In Memory of Fallen Comrades

Delta Company, 17th Infantry Regiment, 1st Logistic, USARV CRB

I dedicate this page to all sons and daughters who lost their lives during war.

17th Infantry Regiment USA Support CMD CRB1st Logistics Command

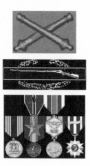 

One tour in Korea Two in Panama, Three tours in Vietnam, Received Bronze Star, Army Commendation, CIB, plus four. 49 months service in Vietnam. Born 9/28/1944 Died 6/24/1972 Age: 28 years

Staff Sergeant George Richard Henson

Sgt Davis & Sp4 McLaren
Campaign Awards & CIB

Sgt Corner Davis (L) Sp4 Robert McLaren (2ndR) 12/25/1939 – 6/23/1972   4/18/1951 – 6/24/1972 Age: 32 years / Age: 21 years

Images & photo of SSG Henson courtesy of *The Virtual Wall,* Please visit www.virtualwall.org — other photos by Richard Alaniz. **Vietnam War**—58,159 service personnel killed (average age 23) 153,329 wounded including 10,000 amputees.

Index

DIVINE
ARTS

HERE ARE OTHER **DIVINE ARTS** BOOKS YOU MAY ENJOY

THE SACRED SITES OF THE DALAI LAMAS
Glenn H. Mullin   2013 Nautilus Silver Medalist

"As this most beautiful book reveals, the Dalai Lamas continue to teach us that there are, indeed, other ways of thinking, other ways of being, other ways of orienting ourselves in social, spiritual, and ecological space.."
— **Wade Davis, Explorer-in-Residence, National Geographic Society**

THE SHAMAN & AYAHUASCA: *Journeys to Sacred Realms*
Don José Campos   2013 Nautilus Silver Medalist

"This remarkable and beautiful book suggests a path back to understand-ing the profound healing and spiritual powers that are here for us in the plant world. This extraordinary book shows a way toward reawakening our respect for the natural world, and thus for ourselves."
— **John Robbins, author, *The Food Revolution* and *Diet for a New America***

A HEART BLOWN OPEN: *The Life & Practice of Zen Master Jun Po Denis Kelly Roshi*
Keith Martin-Smith   2013 Nautilus Silver Medalist

"This is the story of our time... an absolute must-read for anyone with even a passing interest in human evolution..."
— **Ken Wilber, author, *Integral Spirituality***

"This is the legendary story of an inspiring teacher that mirrors the journey of many contemporary Western seekers."
— **Alex Grey, artist and author of *Transfigurations***

SOPHIA—THE FEMININE FACE OF GOD: *Nine Heart Paths to Healing and Abundance*
Karen Speerstra   2013 Nautilus Gold Medalist

"Karen Speerstra shows us most compellingly that when we open our hearts, we discover the wisdom of the Feminine all around us. A totally refreshing exploration, and beautifully researched read."
— **Michael Cecil, author, *Living at the Heart of Creation***

NEW BELIEFS NEW BRAIN: *Free Yourself from Stress and Fear*
Lisa Wimberger

"Lisa Wimberger has earned the right, through trial by fire, to be regarded as a rising star among meditation teachers. No matter where you are in your journey, New Beliefs, New Brain will shine a light on your path."
— **Marianne Williamson, author, *A Return to Love* and *Everyday Grace***

ENERGY WARRIORS: *Overcoming Cancer and Crisis with the Power of Qigong*
Bob Ellal and Lawrence Tan

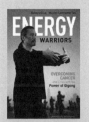

"The combination of Ellal's extraordinary true story and Master Tan's depth of knowledge about the relationship between martial arts and wellness makes for a unique and important contribution to the growing body of literature about holistic thinking and living."
— Jean Benedict Raffa, author, *Healing the Sacred Divide* and *The Bridge to Wholeness*

A FULLER VIEW: *Buckminster Fuller's Vision of Hope and Abundance for All*
L. Steven Sieden

"This book elucidates Buckminster Fuller's thinking, honors his spirit, and creates an enthusiasm for continuing his work."
— Marianne Williamson, author, *Return To Love* and *Healing the Soul of America*

2500 YEARS OF WISDOM: *Sayings of the Great Masters*
D.W. Brown

The wisdom of the greatest minds on earth. All in one place.
This book of carefully selected and arranged quotations represents the greatest philosophical thoughts mankind has produced in its attempt to come to a deeper understanding of the human condition.

WRITING FROM THE INSIDE OUT: *The Practice of Freeform Writing*
Stephen Lloyd Webber

"I urge others to write from the heart to find their true artistic voice. Here is a book that profoundly helps one explore that mysterious personal journey. A navigation guide to our inner creative magic."
— Pen Densham, screenwriter, *Robin Hood: Prince of Thieves* and *Moll Flanders*

CHANGE YOUR STORY, CHANGE YOUR LIFE: *A Path to Success*
Jen Grisanti

"It turns out you can actually get a handle on your life problems by approaching them as an ongoing story that you can rewrite and direct for a better effect."
— Christopher Vogler, author, *The Writer's Journey*

HEAL YOUR SELF WITH WRITING
Catherine Ann Jones

"An elixir for the soul"
— *Psychology Today*

"This is so much more than a book on writing. It is a guide to the soul's journey, with Catherine Ann Jones as a compassionate teacher and wise companion along the way."
— Dr. Betty Sue Flowers, Series Consultant/Editor, *Joseph Campbell and the Power of Myth*

Divine Arts sprang to life fully formed as an intention to bring spiritual practice into daily life.

Human beings are far more than the one-dimensional creatures perceived by most of humanity and held static in consensus reality. There is a deep and vast body of knowledge — both ancient and emerging — that informs and gives us the understanding, through direct experience, that we are magnificent creatures occupying many dimensions with untold powers and connectedness to all that is.

Divine Arts books and films explore these realms, powers, and teachings through inspiring, informative, and empowering works by pioneers, artists, and great teachers from all the wisdom traditions. We invite your participation and look forward to learning how we may serve you.

Onward and upward,
Michael Wiese, Publisher